Family Science

SANDRA MARKLE

WILEY

JOHN WILEY & SONS, INC.

Published by John Wiley & Sons, Inc., Hoboken, New Jersey
Published simultaneously in Canada

Design and composition by Navta Associates, Inc.

The publisher and the author have made every reasonable effort to insure that the experiments and activities in the book are safe when conducted as instructed but assume no responsibility for any damage caused or sustained while performing the experiments or activities in this book. Parents, guardians, and/or teachers should supervise young readers who undertake the experiments and activities in this book.

For general information about our other products and services, please contact our Customer Care Department within the United States at (800) 762-2974, outside the United States at (317) 572-3993 or fax (317) 572-4002.

Wiley also publishes its books in a variety of electronic formats. Some content that appears in print may not be available in electronic books. For more information about Wiley products, visit our web site at www.wiley.com.

Library of Congress Cataloging-in-Publication Data:

Markle, Sandra.
  Family science / Sandra Markle.
     p. cm.
  Includes index.
  ISBN-10 0-471-65197-4 (paper: alk. paper)
  ISBN-13 978-0-471-65197-0 (paper: alk. paper)
  1. Science—Experiments. 2. Science—Study and teaching—Activity programs.
  3. Scientific recreations. I. Title.
  Q164.M2733 2005
  507'.8—dc22
                                                                2004016047

Printed in the United States of America

10 9 8 7 6 5 4 3 2 1

With love for my mother,
Dorothy Haldeman

Contents

Introduction

Why make science activities a family event? First of all, science activities are fun, hands-on projects that family members can enjoy doing together. But even more important, what kids discover by sharing in these activities will help prepare them for life. Science concepts and the scientific inquiry method of tackling problems are basic for helping us understand the world, learn how things function in it, and deal with real-life, everyday situations.

That's why educational experts weren't surprised when a 2004 survey conducted by the U.S. Department of Education showed that an overwhelming majority of parents polled (about 94 percent) were enthusiastic about science and valued science education for their children. However, just a year earlier, the Nation's Report Card—the National Assessment of Educational Progress—had revealed that less than one-third of fourth through eighth graders scored at or above proficient levels in science. The majority of older students scored even more poorly. This clearly demonstrates that for many children, a significant gap exists between what they need to know about basic science concepts and what they've mastered.

Family Science is designed to help parents become mentors, guiding their children to discover and apply science concepts and practice problem-solving skills. *Family Science* activities are completely safe; are easy to do, with simple, step-by-step directions; and are inexpensive to perform because they use readily available materials, many of which can be found around the house. Also, while certain steps in the activities are designed for children to do alone, others specify that they're for children and adults to do together, making each project a clearly shared experience. Although parents will be aware that their children are learning from the activities, the educational lessons are stealthily infused into the play. Kids will likely think of *Family Science* time as family *fun*!

The activities in *Family Science* are divided into seven lively, thematic parts:

1. Science in the Kitchen—Loads of action in the home's kitchen laboratory

2. Science in the Backyard—Expeditions that stay close to home

3. Science in a Minute—Investigations that can be completed in a snap

4. Science Games—Experiments that make investigating fun

5. Science Toys—Activities that use toys to turn science basics into play

6. Science Art—Investigations that are guaranteed to bring out everyone's creative genius

7. Science Contests—Lots of competitive action to spur the home team's inventiveness

Each part is designed to stand alone, so the projects can be done in any order when the time seems right. At the back of the book is a glossary of science words that children may need to know. Each word is also defined when it's first introduced in the book. Within each part, the activities are organized into chapters according to the science concepts being developed: biology, chemistry, or physics. Each activity follows a guided format that makes it easy for you to see at a glance what materials are needed, check out the best strategy for guiding children to successfully and safely complete the activity, and understand before you start what concepts and skills kids will develop from the project. To make this guided format easily accessible, each activity is divided into the following sections:

Fuel Up—The list of materials that will be needed

Blast Off!—A step-by-step list of actions for completing the activity

Brain Booster—An explanation of what happened, why it happened, and the basic science concepts involved

Bonus Pack—Additional activities that provide an opportunity to apply what was discovered

The activities are also designed to include action suitable for children of different ages, as designated by the numbers shown with each activity:

(1) Suitable for preschoolers

(2) Suitable for older children

(3) Suitable for all ages

In addition, you should know a few more things before you get started. Read the following Action Tips and Investigation Safety sections for all the details.

Action Tips

- Read the Fuel Up list for each activity your family will do and collect these items before you start the investigation session. Finding the materials around the house can become a family scavenger hunt, so that it's part of the fun.

- Whenever possible, recycle materials from one activity by using them in another activity.

- Look over the Blast Off! steps before you begin the activity.

- Decide which Blast Off! steps your child is capable of doing alone, which you'll want to share, and which you'll want to perform while your child observes.

- Before reading the Brain Booster section, discuss the activity's results as a family. Consider what was observed and analyze why the results may have happened. Guide children toward drawing realistic conclusions.

- Whenever possible, perform the Bonus Pack activity to apply the concepts that have been introduced.

Investigation Safety

- Be sure that anyone who touches anything that could be hot uses oven mitts.

- Purchase inexpensive plastic safety glasses, such as the kind that home woodworkers use, for each family member. Wear these when specified.

- Always have an adult partner work with a child when using kitchen appliances.

- Instruct children not to put any activity ingredients in their mouths.

- Before sampling the results of any activity, be sure the activity states that the results are edible.

Most of all, be prepared to have fun as a family. *Family Science* is guaranteed to power up your family's creative juices and get everyone involved in investigating the world. That, after all, is what science is all about.

PART I
Science in the Kitchen

Trap gas to bake a tasty treat. Make tarnished silver shine without rubbing it. Trick your taste buds into believing that soggy crackers are apple pie. Make a powder that will fizz on your tongue. Strip an egg naked without touching it. And lots more! The family kitchen is the perfect science laboratory, and there's lots of action ahead. So let's start investigating!

CHAPTER 1

Biology in the Kitchen

Make Monster Beans ③

Young investigators will discover that seeds go through a surprising change to get ready to sprout.

FUEL UP

½ cup dried soup beans, such as great northern beans or pinto beans
empty plastic film container with snap-on lid (or pill container with snap-on lid)
water
paper plate

BLAST OFF!

1. Pour enough soup beans into the container to fill it to the top. Remove just enough so that the lid will snap on.
2. Pour in water to fill the container to the rim and snap on the lid.
3. Set the container on the paper plate and leave overnight.

BRAIN BOOSTER

By the next morning, the beans will have popped the top off the container. Take several out and compare them to a handful of dried soup beans. The beans from the container will be huge monster beans! (Well, they'll be bigger than the dried beans, anyway.) That's because the beans soaked up the water, and the starchy material inside the seed swelled up. If you use a magnifying glass to take a close look at one bean, you'll see a tiny hole on the indented edge. Dried beans are bean

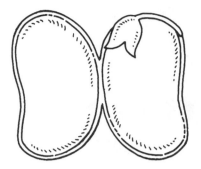

seeds, and they have a tough, protective covering called the seed coat. To sprout and begin to grow, the seeds take in water through the tiny hole in the seed coat. Then they swell, and the seed coat splits open. Carefully separate the two parts of the swollen monster seed, and you'll discover the tiny plant that's ready to start growing.

BONUS PACK

Soak a paper towel in water, squeeze out the excess, and fold the damp towel into fourths. Place the damp towel inside a self-sealing plastic bag. Lay six of the monster beans on the damp towel and seal the bag. Place the bag in a warm spot but not in direct sunlight. Check daily, and you'll soon see the young plants beginning to grow. Once that happens, open the bag, mist with more water, and tape the open bag to a window with masking tape. Mist daily and watch the plants continue to grow. Once green leaves appear, transfer the young plants to flower pots full of potting soil and let them keep on growing.

Or, soak another half cup of beans and add them to your half cup of Monster Beans to whip up a batch of Alphabet Chili (see the recipe in the box on this page).

Alphabet Chili

Fry 1 pound of lean ground beef until it just starts to brown. Stir in ½ cup of minced onion and ½ teaspoon of garlic powder. Brown. Add a cup of soaked beans (any kind of dried beans plus your Monster Beans), ½ teaspoon of chili powder, ½ teaspoon ground cumin, ½ of a cinnamon stick, and salt and pepper to taste. Next, stir in 4 cups of chicken stock (powdered bouillon dissolved in boiling water) and a 16-ounce (453 g) can of chopped peeled tomatoes. Simmer for 1 hour. Meanwhile, cook ½ cup alphabet macaroni in boiling water until tender. Remove the cinnamon stick from the chili mixture, add the alphabet macaroni, and serve.

Create a Juicy T-Shirt ②

Ever wonder how water gets from the soil into the stems and the leaves of a plant? Here's how you can observe this process and put it to work to change a white T-shirt into a colorful creation.

FUEL UP

mordant solution (a chemical solution that prepares the cloth to hold a dyed color—see How to Make Mordant Solution on this page)

plastic bucket

white T-shirt

1 clean 20-ounce (600-ml), or larger, plastic bottle

rubber bands

rubber gloves

1 kitchen juice dye (dyes you make yourself from stuff around the kitchen—see How to Make Kitchen Juice Dyes on page 10)

newspapers

How to Make Mordant Solution

In a large saucepan, combine 1 ounce (28 g) of powdered alum (available in grocery stores) with 1 ounce (28 g) of baking soda. Stir in 4 cups of water, bring to a boil, then reduce the heat to simmer for about 20 minutes. Cool to lukewarm.

BLAST OFF!

Note: This activity can be messy, so wear old clothes and do the soaking steps outdoors.

1. Pour the mordant solution into the bucket. Soak the T-shirt for an hour. Remove and dry. Rinse the bucket. If you want, save the mordant solution in an empty milk jug to reuse with other dying projects.

2. Gather a handful of cloth from the lower half of the front of the T-shirt and twist it. Wrap a rubber band tightly around the twisted cloth to secure it.

3. Repeat, twisting at least three more handfuls of cloth on the front and several on the back of the T-shirt.

4. Slip on the rubber gloves and pour the dye solution into the bucket. Hold the shirt so that the bottom edge is touching the dye solution. Watch as the dye moves up through the cloth.

5. Let the dye continue to climb until it is about halfway up the shirt.

6. Lift the shirt out of the dye and squeeze out any excess dye solution.

7. Without removing the rubber bands, spread the shirt out on newspapers to dry in the sun.

8. After the shirt is dry, rinse it in fresh water and dry again.

9. Remove the rubber bands.

Brain Booster

The water and the dye in it were carried up through the shirt by a process called **capillary action**, the movement of a liquid through a porous material due to the attraction of the liquid to the material and the attraction of the liquid's molecules to each other. This process starts because water **molecules** (the smallest bit of something that can exist and still have all of its characteristics) naturally stick to substances like cloth, soil, and plant tissues. Yet water molecules also tend to stick to each other, so the water molecules stuck to the shirt and moved into the tiny spaces between the fibers. Next, these molecules pulled along more water molecules, and the first molecules climbed higher. Then those molecules dragged along other water molecules, and the water climbed higher up the T-shirt. Did you notice that the water continued to climb up the T-shirt after you removed it from the dye? How high did the water climb before the drying action of water evaporating (escaping into the air from the cloth) stopped it?

Capillary action is essential to green plants because it's how water and minerals move from the soil through the roots and up the stem to the leaves. There, the water helps the plant to produce food.

How to Make Kitchen Juice Dyes

Beet (red) Dye: Drain a can of sliced beets, collecting the juice in a plastic bottle. (Do not use pickled beets—the vinegar dilutes the juice.)

Coffee (brown) Dye: In a saucepan, boil 1 cup of coffee grounds in 1 quart (0.9 l) of water. Continue boiling for 15 minutes. Let it cool and pour the liquid (a kind of matter that has a definite weight but whose shape can change easily) through a strainer into a plastic bottle.

Mustard (yellow) Dye: Scoop ½ cup of prepared American-style yellow mustard into a plastic bottle. Stir in 3 cups of water.

Purple Cabbage (purplish-blue) Dye: In a saucepan, boil 2 cups of chopped purple cabbage in 1 quart (0.9 l) of water. Reduce to a simmer and cook for 30 minutes. Let it cool and pour the liquid through a strainer into a plastic bottle.

BONUS PACK

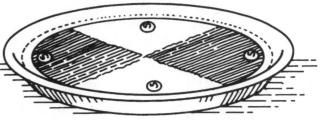

Use capillary action to create candy art. Start by cutting a circle out of a coffee filter. Use a pencil to draw lines dividing the circle into 4 nearly equal slices. Pour just enough water into a pie plate to form a thin layer on the bottom. Next, lay the coffee filter in the water. Place 1 different colored hard candy, such as Skittles or M&Ms, on the edge of each section.

As the candy dissolves, capillary action will spread the candy's coloring through the coffee filter. Surprisingly, the colors will spread out only until they meet. This paints each slice of the paper pie a different color. The reason this happens is that the colors spread out from where the concentration is greatest. When two colors meet, the concentrations are the same, so the spreading stops. If the filter is left in the water, some additional spreading will eventually take place. Or you can take the uniquely colored disk out to dry, and the action will stop.

Make Celery Show Its Stripes ③

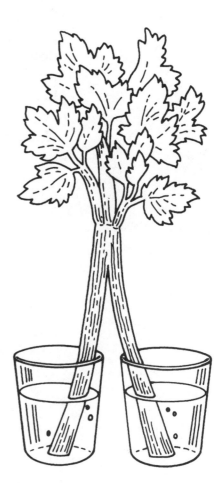

If capillary action worked to dye the T-shirt and also moves water through plants, could you use it to dye a plant? Perform this activity to investigate.

FUEL UP

tall 12-ounce (350-ml) water glass
water
red food coloring
a sturdy stalk leaf-topped celery
kitchen scissors

BLAST OFF!

1. Fill the water glass half full of tap water.

2. Drip in at least 3 drops of red food coloring, enough to make the water turn bright red.

3. Wash the celery stalk and snip off just a little bit of the end that doesn't have any leaves.

4. Place the celery in the glass of colored water, with the trimmed end down.

5. Wait 30 to 60 minutes. Remove the stalk from the water and snip in half lengthwise to expose the celery's red stripes.

6. Munch!

Brain Booster

Celery stalks look solid, but they're really full of strawlike tubes, called xylem (pronounced z-eye-lum) tubes. These tubes transport water from the celery plant's roots to its leaves. Normally, you don't notice the tubes because they're green like the surrounding supporting tissue. But the colored water traveling through the xylem tubes stained them, making them easy to see. Green or red, these tubes have sturdy walls that help strengthen the celery stalks and give them their *crunch*.

Bonus Pack

You can make celery stalk stripes that are two different colors. Use kitchen scissors to snip halfway up the celery stalk before you put it into the colored water. Then fill two glasses nearly full of water. Use food coloring to color one red and the other blue. Set the glasses side by side and place half of the celery stalk in each glass. You may need to set the glasses in the kitchen sink and lean the stalk against the side of the sink to keep it from falling out.

After an hour, snip each half of the celery stalk lengthwise in half again to see the results. Then enjoy your colorful snack.

Could you use this strategy to change the color of a flower—or even make a two-toned flower? Try it and find out.

Get the Water Out ②

Plants are full of water, which makes fruits and vegetables juicy. It's also a problem because water encourages mold growth, making fruits and vegetables rot. This activity introduces a method of getting the water out that's been used to preserve foods since ancient times. In the process, you'll create a shrunken head—an apple head, that is.

Fuel Up

peeler
apple

cutting board
knife (for adult use only)
2 pencils
newspapers or paper towels

Blast Off!

1. Use the peeler to remove the peel from part of the apple. This will become the apple head's face. Leave the peel on the rest of the apple for the head's hair.

2. Have an adult, working on the cutting board, cut away sections on the face to give the head a nose, eye sockets, and a mouth.

3. Have an adult insert the writing end of one pencil into the bottom of the apple.

4. Use the other pencil's eraser end to push against the apple's flesh to finish shaping the facial features.

5. Set the apple on newspapers or paper towels in a sunny place.

6. Be patient and wait 1 week before checking your apple head.

Brain Booster

The apple head has shrunk, and the face appears to have shriveled with age. That's because the apple has lost much of its natural moisture, but it won't be rotten or moldy. One way that people have always preserved food for use during the winter was to dry it. The lower moisture content discourages bacteria and mold growth.

Bonus Pack

Use tissue paper or cloth scraps to make clothes and turn the apple head into an apple doll. In the United States during pioneer times, children sometimes played with apple-head dolls.

Or make a popular old-time treat—apple leather. Start with 4 cups of applesauce. Add 4 tablespoons of honey to help keep the fruit leather flexible once it's dried. Use a cookie sheet with a raised edge all the way around to prevent spillage. Line this with plastic wrap. Spread the fruit and honey mixture in a thin layer about ¼-inch (0.62-cm) thick. Set the oven to 140°F (60°C), place the cookie sheet in the oven, leave the oven door open a couple of inches, and let the mixture dry for about 4 hours. The apple leather is dry enough when a corner can be lifted and peeled back easily. Remove from the oven and let it cool completely. Then roll it up—plastic wrap and all—to store it. Apple leather can be kept at room temperature for about a month or much longer in the refrigerator. Slice it into pieces to unroll and eat.

Mummify Steak ②

Now, let's investigate another way to get the water out of food. This method was even used by the ancient Egyptians to prepare their mummies.

FUEL UP

palm-sized piece of flank steak, round steak, or any thin, inexpensive steak
baking pan
cutting board
knife (for adult use only)
salt

BLAST OFF!

1. Wash your hands with soap and water before beginning. Be sure all of your equipment is clean.

2. Rinse the meat in cool water. Put it on the baking pan and bake in the oven at 160°F (71°C) for about 10 minutes or until the meat is cooked through.

3. Take the baking pan out of the oven, let the meat cool, and place it on the cutting board. Wash and dry the baking pan.

4. Have an adult cut slits in the upper surface of the meat.

5. Cover the bottom of the baking pan with salt. Place the meat on the salt and completely cover with more salt.

6. Place the baking pan in an oven set to 140°F (60°C), keep the oven door open a crack, and leave the meat in the oven for about 4 hours or until it is completely dried out.

BRAIN BOOSTER

You've just prepared what's nicknamed beef jerky. Be sure to brush off the salt crust before eating the jerky. Drying is an ancient way of preserving meat that goes back to the ancient Egyptians. It preserves the meat by removing moisture that could encourage bacteria and mold growth. Cooking the meat before drying it helps to ensure that any bacteria present are killed before you start the preserving process. Jerky is also lighter and easier to carry along than fresh meat, so it's been popular with travelers for centuries. Native Americans used to mix dried meat with dried fruit and suet (fat) to make what they called pemmican.

Bonus Pack

The ancient Egyptians used a similar method to preserve human bodies, creating mummies. For this process, they used a special salt mixture called natron. You can mix up natron by combining ½ cup of baking soda, ½ cup of a powdered laundry bleach that contains sodium carbonate, and ½ cup of table salt. Pour the natron mixture into a plastic mixing bowl, then bury a piece of meat in it and let it set. Check after a week and continue checking until the meat is dried up. The mummified meat is *not* edible, but compare its appearance and texture to the beef jerky you prepared. According to ancient records, it took about 70 days to mummify a human body. Of course, Egypt's hot, dry climate helped.

Or you can make a salt dough that won't mold and can be used to create refrigerator art. Mix together 1 cup of flour, ½ cup of table salt, 2 teaspoons of cream of tartar, and 1 cup of water. Have an adult cook this over medium heat, stirring until it's thick and smooth. Cool and knead in a drop or two of vegetable oil to help make it more moldable. Then use the dough to create interesting shapes, such as small flowers or pretend cakes. Press a small magnet into the soft dough. When the sculpture has hardened, coat it with craft varnish and let it dry. Then stick it to the refrigerator as a decorative note holder.

Grow Monster Bean Sprouts ③

Find out what extremes green plants will go to in their search for the light energy they need to produce food.

Fuel Up

12 dried soup beans, such as great northern beans (select only whole beans)
bowl
water
pencil
3 Styrofoam cups
potting soil
clear plastic wrap
gift or packing box about a foot square

Blast Off!

1. Place the beans in the bowl, cover with water, and let set overnight.

2. Use the pencil's point to poke 3 holes in the bottom of each cup.

3. Fill each cup two-thirds full of potting soil.

4. Push 4 soaked beans into the soil in each cup. Lightly cover with soil.

5. Sprinkle water on the soil and cover each cup with clear plastic wrap.

6. Place one cup on a warm, sunny windowsill. Place another cup in the same room but somewhere that the light is dim, such as in a corner behind a chair. Place the third cup in the same room and cover it with the overturned box.

7. Every third day, uncover the cups just long enough to sprinkle the soil with water.

8. Watch for a week after sprouts appear.

Brain Booster

While the plants grown in the sunshine and in dim light looked normal, the sprouts developing in the dark became long, thin, and pale. Seeds contain stored food that fuels a young plant's initial growth. To continue to grow, green plants need to produce their own food by combining water from the soil and carbon dioxide from the air during a process called **photosynthesis** that is powered by the sun's light energy. When exposed to sunlight, plants produce a special green **pigment** or coloring matter, called **chlorophyll** (the green coloring matter produced in plants), to trap the sun's energy. Without sunlight, young plants remain pale. Using up their stored energy to generate stem growth, they also grow long and thin. Normally, this increases the sprout's chances to reach sunlight. Your sprouts growing in dim light are likely to be longer and thinner than those growing in the sunny window.

BONUS PACK

Sprout a new set of seeds under the box. This time, though, cut a ping-pong-ball-sized hole in the box. Watch to see if the plants can meet the challenge of growing toward this light source. Do any of the plants eventually grow out through the hole?

Or, grow your own sproutwich. Sprouts are a popular food, and sprouts grown in the dark are thought to be more tender and tasty. Here's how to do it:

1. Purchase seeds that are described as being especially for producing sprouts, such as mung beans, alfalfa, or barley seeds from a health food store.

2. Line a colander or a strainer with a piece of muslin cloth or a sturdy paper towel. Put the seeds in this. Rinse the seeds.

3. Place the rinsed seeds in a quart-sized (liter-sized) jar. Cover the top with another piece of muslin cloth or a piece of clean (unused) nylon stocking material. Secure with a rubber band.

4. Keep the jar in a dark place. Each day, remove the cover, rinse, and drain the seeds again.

5. Sprouts will appear in about 3 to 5 days. Once most of the seeds have sprouted, rinse and drain them. Then add grated cheese and chopped egg or vegetables, such as tomato or avocado. Tuck the mixture into a pita pocket and enjoy.

Make Yeast Blow Up a Balloon ①

What a way for kids to discover that even tiny organisms, like yeast, give off a waste gas! Before starting, pour the contents of a package of baker's yeast into a bowl. Brainstorm what might be needed to make the yeast grow, such as food, water, and being warm. Then follow the directions to see what happens when the yeast starts to grow.

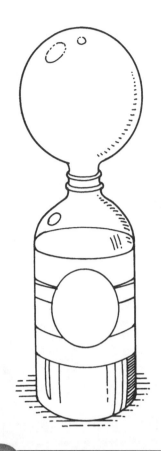

FUEL UP

1 package yeast
empty 20-ounce clear plastic water bottle (600 ml or larger)
1 teaspoon sugar
½ cup lukewarm tap water
round rubber balloon

BLAST OFF!

1. Carefully pour the yeast into the empty plastic bottle.
2. Pour in the sugar and the water.
3. Gently tip the bottle back and forth to mix.
4. Slip the neck of the balloon over the bottle's mouth.
5. Check the size of the balloon every 15 minutes for an hour.

BONUS PACK

Use yeast to make a fun, yummy bread. See the Peanutty Rolls recipe in the box on this page.

Peanutty Rolls

In a mixing bowl combine 1 package of yeast, 2 tablespoons of sugar, and ½ teaspoon of salt. In a saucepan, heat ½ cup of milk and ¼ cup of crunchy peanut butter until warm. Add to the dry ingredients. Use an electric mixer to stir in 1½ cups of flour. Put the dough on a floured cutting board. Slowly sprinkle on more flour and knead until the dough is smooth and elastic. Place the dough in a greased mixing bowl. Cover with paper towels and let it rise in a warm place for about an hour. Divide dough into egg-sized lumps and roll into balls. Place on a greased cookie sheet, cover with paper towels, and let the balls rise for about 1 hour. Bake at 350°F (180°C) for 10 minutes or until golden brown. Cool, slice, fill with jelly, and eat.

Don't worry that you're eating living yeast or alcohol. Baking kills the yeast and makes the alcohol turn into a gas that escapes into the air.

BRAIN BOOSTER

Once the sugar became warm and wet, the yeast used it as food and began to grow. During the process, the yeast gave off carbon dioxide gas and a kind of alcohol as waste products. The gas bubbled up and escaped until it was trapped by the balloon. Slowly, the gas inflated the balloon. The balloon will never inflate as fully as it would if you blew into it, but you may be surprised by how much the trapped gas will inflate the balloon.

THAT'S AMAZING

Yeast is a tiny organism that can be found wild in the soil and even in the air. Although bakers in ancient Egypt didn't know about yeast, they knew that letting their dough set exposed to the air would make it start to rise. Today, we know that these early bakers were catching wild yeast that blew through the air.

Raise Brine Shrimps ②

Here's your family's chance to observe wildlife in the kitchen. Before launching this activity, consider what conditions these aquatic animals will likely need to live. As the activity continues, make a family journal—complete with pictures—recording how the animals change and behave as they grow up.

FUEL UP

2 identical 20-ounce (600-ml), or larger, clear plastic bottles filled with water
measuring cup
mixing bowl
aquarium salt
brine shrimp (*Artemia franciscana*) eggs (available at pet and aquarium stores)
magnifying glass (if you have one)
*yeast (this is used in the Brain Booster activity)

BLAST OFF!

1. Pour water from one bottle into the mixing bowl a cup at a time, keeping track of how many cupfuls are used.

2. Add 1 tablespoon of aquarium salt per cup of water. Stir to dissolve and pour the salt water back into the bottle.

3. Repeat to add salt to the second water bottle. Cap this bottle and set it aside for the Brain Booster activity.

4. Add a pinch of brine shrimp eggs to the uncapped bottle. Place it in a warm spot but not in direct sun.

5. Check every day. If you have a magnifying glass available, use it to help you get a better view.

Brain Booster

Because you supplied the right conditions, the eggs will hatch in 3 to 5 days. Then you'll see newly hatched brine shrimps. These will appear as tiny active orange spots. Watch and add more water from the capped bottle as needed to keep the brine shrimps' home full. Feed with a few grains of yeast about twice a week. In about 6 days, the young shrimps will mature into adults that have lots of legs and appear to glide through the water. Within 2 to 3 weeks, the adults will mate, and you'll be able to identify the females by the eggs in their bellies. Female brine shrimps each produce over a hundred eggs every 3 to 4 days. These will hatch, multiplying the critters in your bottle. The adults live about 6 months.

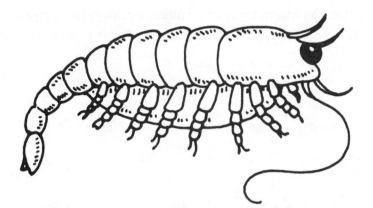

Bonus Pack

Conduct tests to find out how different conditions affect the brine shrimps. Design your own tests or try these:

- Observe how they behave in bright light and in dim light.
- Observe how they behave in extra salty water by adding another tablespoon of aquarium salt.
- Observe how they behave when chilled by placing the container in the refrigerator for 5 minutes.

You may want to see how long your brine shrimp colony will keep on going. Or you can add vinegar until all activity stops. Then dispose of the remains by pouring the contents of the bottle down the drain.

Trick Your Tongue ②

A kitchen is the perfect place to investigate how the senses of smell and taste work together.

FUEL UP

diced very sharp cheddar cheese (one cube per person)
diced tofu (one cube per person)

BLAST OFF!

1. Take turns taking this test.
2. The people being tested will need to keep their eyes shut and pinch their noses between their fingers.
3. The helper should use a fork to place one taste cube—either the sharp cheese or the tofu—on each test taker's tongue.
4. Without taking a breath, each test taker should try to judge which cube is on his or her tongue.
5. Then each test taker should release his or her nose, take a deep breath, and guess again.
6. Switch places so that everyone has a chance to be both helper and test taker.

Brain Booster

Your senses of smell and taste work together to give food flavor. The taste buds on your tongue are able to detect only whether food is bitter, salty, sweet, or sour. Then they send messages to your brain. But your brain also receives more complex messages about the smell of food. Scents given off by food are carried on the air you breathe into your nasal passages, where sensors detect them and transmit lots more messages to the brain. Most people can detect from 4,000 to 10,000 different scent messages. When your brain analyzes both sets of messages, it makes you aware of the flavor in your mouth. Of course, this happens almost instantly. If you have your nose closed, however, your brain receives messages only from the taste buds. Then foods like cheese and tofu will likely taste pretty much the same.

That's Amazing

Houseflies have odor-sensitive cells on their feet. Imagine smelling everything that you step on!

Bonus Pack

Put your smell memory to the test. Collect plastic film containers with snap-on lids or use self-sealing plastic bags. Soak cotton balls in a variety of juices and cooking essences, such as lemon, chocolate, lime, almond, orange, and so forth. Put one soaked cotton ball in each container and seal. Number each bag with a permanent marker. Make a master list of the numbered bags and which scent they contain. Take turns opening the bags and sniffing. How many scents can each person identify?

CHAPTER 2

Chemistry in the Kitchen

Launch Spaghetti Rockets ①

Investigate the chemical reaction that happens when two different kinds of chemicals—acids and bases—interact. Before you start, explain that weak **acids** are found in many foods like fruit juices and tea. They give these foods a sharp taste. **Bases** are used in many cleaning products because they're naturally slippery and soapy. However, one base, baking soda, is used in foods.

FUEL UP

1 teaspoon baking soda
2-inch (5-cm) square piece of toilet paper
tall 12-ounce (350-ml), or larger, water glass
4 dried spaghetti noodles
2 cups white vinegar

BLAST OFF!

1. Spoon the baking soda onto the paper. Roll up the paper and twist the ends shut.

2. Place the paper packet in the bottom of the glass.

3. Break the spaghetti into 1-inch (2.5-cm) pieces, and place them on top of the paper packet.

4. Pour the vinegar into the glass.

5. Once the paper breaks down, watch the spaghetti bits zoom up, drift down, and soar again.

Brain Booster

When the baking soda, a base, combined with the vinegar, an acid, a chemical reaction happened, and bubbles of carbon dioxide gas were released. These bubbles stuck to the surface of the spaghetti noodles. Watch closely, and you'll see bubbles build up until there is almost a solid bubble coat on each bit of pasta. Then the spaghetti pieces zoom up as the bubbles burst after being exposed to air. When there are no longer enough gas bubbles to support the weight of the spaghetti, the pieces sink. Then the bubbles begin to re-stick to the spaghetti, and the action starts all over.

Bonus Pack

Eventually, all of the baking soda will have reacted with the vinegar, and no more gas bubbles will be produced. Could adding more baking soda launch the spaghetti rockets again? Add a tablespoonful to find out.

Carbonated drinks cause this same kind of bubble reaction. Repeat the experiment, filling 3 glasses with different carbonated drinks to decide which one produces the most bubbles. This time, the carbon dioxide in the drink replaces the gas produced by an acid reacting with baking soda. Does the drink's temperature affect how bubbly it is? Develop a test to find out.

Strip an Egg Naked without Touching It ③

Find out what happens when vinegar, a weak fruit acid, interacts with an egg's shell, a **solid**, a kind of matter with a definite weight and whose shape can't change easily.

Fuel Up

> 1 uncooked egg
> tall 12-ounce (350-ml) water glass
> vinegar

Blast Off!

1. Place the egg in the glass.
2. Pour in enough vinegar to cover the egg.

3. Let the egg sit in the vinegar for about 3 days, or until the shell rolls off when you rub the egg with your fingers.

Brain Booster

The vinegar dissolved or broke down and suspended the calcium carbonate, the main chemical in the egg's hard shell. Some of the calcium carbonate will have naturally moved into the vinegar solution. Rubbing gently removes the rest. However, the vinegar did not break down the tough membrane that was just inside the shell, so the egg is still intact. You can hold this naked egg in your hand. Hold it up to a light and check out the yolk inside.

Bonus Pack

Repeat this activity by soaking a clean chicken bone in vinegar for a week. The bone will become rubbery because, like the egg, it's mainly made up of calcium carbonate.

Bake Foam You Can Eat ②

Here's a tasty way for you to discover that when an acid interacts with a base, the reaction releases a gas. Making a batter that traps the gas will produce foods that are light and fluffy.

Fuel Up

electric mixer
¼ cup margarine
1 cup sugar
mixing bowl
1 egg
1½ teaspoons cinnamon
1 teaspoon baking soda
¼ teaspoon salt
2 cups flour
1¼ cups applesauce
spoon
¼ cup chocolate chips
paper baking cups
muffin tin

Blast Off!

1. Preheat the oven to 350°F (180°C).

2. Using an electric mixer, cream together the margarine and sugar in the mixing bowl.

3. Add the egg and beat.

4. Mix in the dry ingredients and the applesauce.

5. Use the spoon to stir in the chocolate chips.

6. Place paper baking cups in the muffin tin and fill each cup two-thirds full.

7. Bake for 15 minutes or until golden brown.

Brain Booster

The baking soda reacted with the applesauce mixture, producing carbon dioxide gas. Applesauce, like many foods, naturally contains a weak form of acid. Acids give foods that contain them a sharp or even slightly bitter taste. Baking soda is another kind of chemical called a base. When bases and acids are combined, they react. This reaction produces carbon dioxide gas. Because the gas bubbles were trapped by the sticky batter, they made the batter foam, causing it to expand and rise. Muffins and other types of cake dough are actually foam that has solidified. As the batter bakes, it dries but holds its shape. The gas bubbles form all the little holes in muffins or cakes.

Bonus Pack

Bend a 3-by-5-inch (7.5-by-12.5-cm) index card or a piece of poster board into a funnel and staple the edges together. Working over the sink, fill the funnel two-thirds full of baking soda. Cap it with a sturdy paper plate. Turn the funnel and plate over and set it in the sink. Use scissors to snip off the funnel's tip, creating an opening about as big around as your index finger. In a mixing cup, add 5 drops of red food coloring to ¼ cup of vinegar. Pour the vinegar into the top of the funnel. When the baking soda and the acid react by producing carbon dioxide gas, the result will be volcanic.

Make a Mouth Bomb ②

Discover that chemical reactions won't happen until conditions are right. In this case, the interacting chemicals are activated when they **dissolve**, or break up into smaller bits. The reaction is a tongue tickler.

FUEL UP

- 1 tablespoon baking soda
- 2 tablespoons Ever-Fresh powder or any fruit preserver with citric acid (used to keep sliced fruit from darkening)
- 1 envelope sweetened, fruit-flavored gelatin
- mixing bowl
- self-sealing plastic bag
- spoon
- *glass of water (this is used in the Brain Booster activity)

BLAST OFF!

1. Mix all of the ingredients together in the bowl.
2. Store in the self-sealing plastic bag.
3. To experience a mouth bomb, scoop about a half teaspoonful onto your tongue and close your mouth.

BRAIN BOOSTER

The tingle you feel is from a chemical reaction. When the moisture in your mouth dissolved the chemicals, the citric acid in the fruit preserver and the flavored gelatin reacted with the base, the baking soda. That produced carbon dioxide gas bubbles. If you want to see these bubbles and make a tasty drink, mix 1 tablespoon of the powder in a glass of water.

BONUS PACK

Mix up bath bombs for fizzy fun in the bathtub. In a bowl, mix together ½ cup of Ever-Fresh powder or any fruit preserver with citric acid (used to keep sliced fruit from darkening), ½ cup of cornstarch, 1 cup of baking soda, 2 teaspoons of orange essence (available in grocery stores) or use the same amount of citric essential oil (available from stores that sell soaps and bath products), 6 drops of any food coloring, and 3 tablespoons of sunflower oil.

Drop teaspoonfuls of this mixture onto waxed paper and let them harden. Put one or more of these colorful bombs into your bath to start the fizzing reaction and release the scent.

Create Fake Flavors ③

Investigate how chemicals can simulate the unique flavors of foods, such as apples. There aren't any apples in this mock apple pie, but your taste buds will think there are.

FUEL UP

36 Ritz crackers
premade pie crust in aluminum pan
water
saucepan
spoon
1½ cups granulated sugar
1½ teaspoons cream of tartar
2 tablespoons lemon juice
oven mitts
½ teaspoon cinnamon
4 tablespoons margarine
¼ cup flour
¼ cup brown sugar
fork
cooling rack

BLAST OFF!

1. Preheat the oven to 350°F (180°C).

2. Wash and dry your hands. Break up the crackers and spread the chunks on top of the pie crust.

3. Pour 2 cups of water into the saucepan. Stir in the granulated sugar and cream of tartar.

4. Bring to a boil. Then reduce the heat and simmer for 15 minutes or until the sauce thickens.

5. Stir in the lemon juice.

6. Have an adult use oven mitts to take the pan off the stove and pour the sauce over the crackers. Sprinkle on the cinnamon and dot with 2 tablespoons of the margarine.

7. In the saucepan combine the remaining margarine, the flour, and the brown sugar. Mix with a fork until crumbly.

8. Spoon the crumbly sugar mixture over the pie filling.

9. Bake 30 minutes or until the crust is golden brown.

10. Have an adult use oven mitts to transfer the pie to the cooling rack. Cool and eat.

BRAIN BOOSTER

On your tongue, the texture of the crackers felt like cooked apples. The cream of tartar and the lemon juice are both weak acids. They combined with the sugar and the cinnamon to simulate the sweet-tart, spicy taste of apple pie. Artificial flavors are commonly used in foods and even in chewing gum. Sometimes, it's easier and cheaper to produce an artificial flavoring than real fruit flavors. In 1933, the National Biscuit Company developed the Ritz cracker and shortly after that introduced the recipe for Mock Apple Pie. This became a popular fake dessert during World War II, when fresh apples were scarce and expensive.

BONUS PACK

While the Coca-Cola recipe is a carefully guarded secret, you can mix together the following flavorings to produce your own version of this popular drink. Vary the amounts of each ingredient to make the drink more to your personal taste.

Home-Brew Cola

In a saucepan, mix 3 ounces (88 ml) of lime juice, 2 tablespoons of clear corn syrup, 2 tablespoons of chocolate syrup, 1 tablespoon of caramel sauce (for ice cream), 1 teaspoon of instant coffee crystals, a pinch each of nutmeg and cinnamon, 1 teaspoon of orange essence, 1 teaspoon of lemon essence, and 1 tablespoon of vanilla into 4 cups of water. Bring to a boil, let it cool, and serve over ice.

Make Silver Shine without Touching It ②

Discover that a chemical reaction can cause **matter** (any substance or material) to change form. Also investigate how chemicals in the air can cause a chemical change.

Fuel Up

heavy-duty aluminum foil
large metal saucepan
1 to 5 tarnished silver pieces, such as knives, forks, spoons, candlesticks, or jewelry
water
oven mitts
½ cup baking soda

Blast Off!

1. Tear off a sheet of foil about a yard (0.9-m) long and use it, shiny side up, to line the bottom and sides of the saucepan. Fold any extra so that it fits inside the pan

2. Place the silver pieces on the foil.

3. Fill the pan two-thirds full of water or full enough to cover the silver pieces.

4. Bring the water to a boil. Have an adult use oven mitts to move the pan to the sink.

5. Pour in the baking soda. *Be careful. The water will foam and may spill over the sides of the saucepan.*

6. Let the water cool completely before removing the silver pieces for a close look.

Brain Booster

The silver has become shiny! Silver gets tarnished when the surface molecules react with sulfur and form silver sulfide. And silver can come into contact with sulfur in a lot of places, including from people's hands or even being exposed to air. Rubbing the silver with polish makes it shine because you rub off the silver sulfide, but you also rub off some of the silver molecules. If you use the chemical reaction with baking soda water, silver sulfide is transformed back into silver, and the sulfur is freed.

Sulfur is even more strongly attracted to aluminum than to silver. As long as the silver is in contact with the foil, the sulfur is transferred to the aluminum. Heat makes the reaction happen faster.

BONUS PACK

Ready for more bubbling action? Try this. Set a tall 12-ounce (350-ml) water glass in the sink. Pour in 1 tablespoon of powdered laundry detergent, 1 tablespoon of baking soda, and 3 drops of red food coloring. In a 2-cup measuring cup, combine ¾ cup of water and ¼ cup of vinegar. Pour this solution into the water glass as well. The solution will fizz, and foam will pour over the sides. The baking soda and the vinegar are reacting to produce carbon dioxide gas. The gas is then trapped by the soapy liquid, which creates foam.

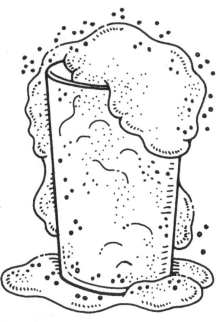

Stick Oil and Vinegar Together ③

To get started, pour 4 tablespoons of white vinegar and 1 cup of vegetable oil into a clean 12-ounce (about 350-ml) glass. Whip briskly with a fork and watch what happens. The two liquids will quickly separate. The next investigation demonstrates how introducing another substance—egg yolk—can make one liquid stay suspended in the other when they normally would separate. What you'll create is a familiar, tasty food.

FUEL UP

4 tablespoons white vinegar
clean 12-ounce (350-ml) glass
1 cup vegetable oil
whisk
1 egg yolk (Have an adult partner help separate the white from the yolk.)
mixing bowl

BLAST OFF!

1. Pour 2 tablespoons of vinegar into the glass.

2. Add the vegetable oil and whisk for a count of five.

3. Let the vinegar and oil sit for 2 minutes, then look through the side of the glass. You'll see that the two liquids have separated, with the less thick vinegar settling on top of the denser oil.

4. An adult partner will need to help separate the egg yolk from the egg white, dropping the yolk into the mixing bowl and saving the white for scrambled eggs or another recipe.

5. Whisk the yolk. Then add the vinegar and oil to the mixing bowl and whisk again until the result looks smooth and creamy.

Brain Booster

When you tried to combine the oil and the vinegar, the two liquids first broke into lots of tiny droplets that were mixed together. Then the oil droplets joined into bigger droplets. The tiny vinegar droplets did the same thing. Soon there was an oil layer and a vinegar layer, and the denser oil sank below the less dense vinegar. Whisking in the egg broke the oil and vinegar into tiny droplets again and coated each one with yolk. This kept the oil droplets from joining with other oil droplets and the vinegar droplets from joining with other vinegar droplets. So the two liquids plus the egg yolk remained a mixture of tiny droplets. Taste what you just whipped up. You've created mayonnaise.

Bonus Pack

You may want to add a pinch of salt and stir in ¼ teaspoon of mustard to give your mayonnaise added flavor. Spread it on bread and enjoy it alone or with a slice of tomato or cheese.

Shake Up Butter ①

Now, investigate how to get one kind of dissolved matter to separate out.

Fuel Up

clean glass jar with a screw-on lid, such as a small salad dressing jar
whipping cream

Blast Off!

1. Fill the jar half full of whipping cream.

2. Screw on the lid tightly.

3. Take turns shaking the jar back and forth rapidly until yellow flakes appear. Depending on the shaking action, this can take from 5 to 20 minutes.

4. Keep shaking until the jar contains a yellow solid and a liquid.

5. Drain the liquid into a glass.

Brain Booster

The cream separated into fat (butter) and buttermilk. The shaking made the flakes of fat clump together. When the clumps were big enough, they became too heavy to remain suspended in the liquid.

Bonus Pack

Use cold water to rinse off the butter. Add a pinch of salt and mix in a little honey. Then spread it on bread or crackers for a tasty treat. You may want to try a taste of the liquid, too. It's buttermilk.

Turn Glue into Glubber  ②

Watch how runny, liquid glue changes when this chemical reaction makes the glue molecules link together into chains.

Fuel Up

spoon
1 tablespoon borax soap (available in the laundry soap section of grocery stores)
2 paper cups
¼ cup water
¼ cup white glue (Elmer's Glue-All or Elmer's School Glue works best)

Blast Off!

1. Use the spoon to scoop the borax into one paper cup, then pour in the water.

2. Stir until most of the borax is dissolved.

3. Pour the glue into the second cup.

4. Add the borax solution to the glue, leaving any crystals that didn't dissolve in the bottom of the cup.

5. Stir the borax solution into the glue until a solid lump forms.

6. Working over the kitchen sink, scoop this lump into your hands. With the tap running, squeeze the solid lump to get out any trapped liquid glue and rinse it away. Continue until no more liquid glue runs out.

7. Pat it dry with the paper towel and squeeze to shape into a ball—glubber.

8. Drop the glubber on the floor. What happens?

BRAIN BOOSTER

The glubber bounced. What you created is a substance known as a **polymer**. While all matter is made up of building blocks called molecules, polymers have their molecules linked together. Often polymers, like the glue, are made up of long chains of linked molecules. In this case, the borax soap is a substance that binds the glue's molecule chains together, creating a stronger, thicker polymer material. One of this material's properties is to be rubbery enough to bounce. Test the glubber to determine what other properties it has. For example, can it be stretched? Does it hold its shape? Can it be easily broken into two pieces?

BONUS PACK

Go on a polymer hunt around the house. Look for things that are made of or that contain these common polymers: plastic, nylon, polyester, rayon, Teflon (nonstick coating on cooking and baking pans), polystyrene (called Styrofoam), and Formica.

Make Your Own Marshmallows ②

Marshmallows are actually polymers—chains of molecules. Before you start whipping some up, role-play what will happen in this activity. Have each family member pretend to be a molecule, a building block of matter. Have all of the molecules circle one leader while you count to five. Then, on your signal, have everyone join hands to form a chain. Now that you know what the molecular structure of marshmallows is like, follow the steps to make some of these yummy polymers.

Fuel Up

2 mixing bowls
¼ cup cornstarch
⅓ cup powdered confectionery sugar
8-by-8-inch square glass or metal baking pan
cooking oil spray
water
saucepan
1 package unflavored gelatin
⅔ cup granulated sugar
oven mitts
½ cup light corn syrup
pinch of salt
1 teaspoon vanilla
electric mixer

Blast Off!

1. In one of the bowls, mix together the cornstarch and powdered sugar.

2. Spray the baking pan with the oil. Dust with about a tablespoon of the cornstarch and sugar mixture.

3. Pour ⅓ cup of water into the saucepan.

4. Sprinkle in the gelatin. Let it soak for about 5 minutes.

5. Add the granulated sugar. Cook over low heat until the gelatin and sugar dissolve.

6. Have an adult use oven mitts to pour the gelatin mixture into the second mixing bowl.

7. Add the corn syrup, salt, and vanilla.

8. Using an electric mixer, beat on high for 15 minutes or until peaks form.

9. Spread the mixture into the greased and dusted pan.

10. Let the mixture set for 2 hours or until firm to the touch.

11. Sprinkle the top with more of the remaining cornstarch and sugar mixture.

12. Cut it into blocks and roll each block in the remaining cornstarch and sugar mixture.

13. Eat some of your polymer.

Brain Booster

The gelatin is the polymer in this recipe. When it's dissolved, the chains are free-floating. When mixed with the sugary solution and cooled, the gelatin chains form a tangled web, trapping the sugary liquid in tiny gaps. That's what gives a marshmallow its familiar springy texture.

Amazingly, the ancient Egyptians are credited with inventing marshmallows. They made a puffy white treat by combining honey with the sap of the carrot-shaped root of the marsh mallow plant. Candy makers began to produce the first gelatin-based marshmallows in the 1800s.

Bonus Pack

Make more marshmallows, but this time add a fruit essence, such as lemon essence, and food coloring to make special, colorful treats.

Use Salt to Lift an Ice Cube ③

Investigate how salt affects water's freezing point. What happens looks like magic!

Fuel Up

a piece of sewing thread or yarn
glass of water
ice cube
table salt

Blast Off!

1. Dip one end of the thread or yarn in the glass of water.
2. Use your fingers to squeeze the excess water out of the thread.
3. Coil the wet end of the thread onto the ice cube.
4. Sprinkle salt over the coiled thread.
5. Slowly count to 20, then gently pull straight up on the thread.

BRAIN BOOSTER

The thread has stuck to the ice, so when you tugged the string, you lifted the cube into the air. This happened because water normally freezes at 32°F (0°C). However, salt water won't freeze until the temperature is lower. Placing salt on ice makes the ice melt unless the surrounding air temperature is lower than 32°F (0°C). To melt, ice needs heat energy, and it takes that heat energy from any warmer matter that it's in contact with—such as the water on the wet thread. While the surface of the cube melted, enough heat was removed from the thread to make the water on its fibers freeze. The ice glaze made the thread stick to the ice cube.

BONUS PACK

Will sugar lower the freezing temperature of water the same way that salt does? Try freezing fruit pops to find out. Mix together 1 tablespoon of grape juice concentrate and 1 cup of water. Pour into paper cups until each is about half full. Half fill identical paper cups with plain water. Set all of the cups in a metal cake pan in the freezer. Check after 10 minutes and then every 10 minutes until at least one of the cups is frozen solid. You'll discover that sugar, including natural fruit sugar, dissolved in water, lowers water's freezing point.

Use Salt to Freeze a Watermelon Treat ③

Whip up another taste treat by using salt to affect the freezing temperature of water.

FUEL UP

    nail
    hammer
    plastic bucket
    measuring cup
    4 cups watermelon puree (whip in a blender or crush with a potato masher)
    saucepan
    1 tablespoon unflavored gelatin
    large mixing bowl
    1 cup powdered confectionery sugar

1½ teaspoons lemon juice
1½ cups light cream
clean, empty quart (liter) jar with screw-on lid
crushed ice
spoon
rock salt
oven mitts
long-handled spoon

BLAST OFF!

1. Have an adult use the nail and hammer to punch 6 holes in the bottom of the plastic bucket.

2. Scoop ½ cup of watermelon puree into the saucepan.

3. Sprinkle the gelatin on the watermelon and let it soak in for 5 minutes. Heat it on low, stirring just until the gelatin dissolves.

4. Let the gelatin mixture cool.

5. In the mixing bowl, combine the powdered sugar, lemon juice, and light cream. Stir in the gelatin mixture.

6. Scoop the watermelon mixture into the jar and screw on the lid.

7. Set the bucket in the kitchen sink. Pour a layer of crushed ice into the bottom. Use the spoon to sprinkle rock salt over the ice.

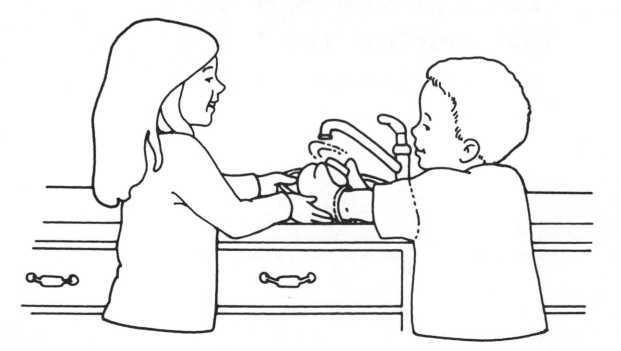

8. Set the jar in the center of the bucket. Pack crushed ice into the bucket until it's about halfway up the sides of the jar. Sprinkle on more rock salt to cover the surface of the ice. Continue adding ice until it is about 2 inches (5 cm) below the jar's lid.

9. Put on the oven mitts. Have a partner hold the bucket while you grip the jar lid. Twist the jar around and around.

10. Every 5 minutes, unscrew the lid and have a partner use the long-handled spoon to stir the watermelon ice. Then screw on the lid again and keep twisting the jar.

11. As the ice melts and the water drains away, pour fresh ice into the bucket and sprinkle with more rock salt.

12. Continue for about 20 minutes or until the watermelon mixture is thick.

13. Serve and eat.

Brain Booster

The melting process drew heat energy away from the watermelon mixture. That lowered the water-melon mixture's temperature enough to transform it into a thick, soft, frozen treat.

That's Amazing

It's believed that the first ice cream was served in ancient Rome. Emperor Nero had slaves run a relay race into nearby mountains and bring back fresh snow, which was mixed with fruit, wine, or honey to make a frosty treat.

Bonus Pack

Following these directions, young children can use the same salt-ice reaction to shake up an ice cream snack on their own. Each child will need: a gallon-sized (4.5-l) self-sealing plastic bag, a quart-sized (1-l) self-sealing plastic bag, oven mitts, ¼ cup of powdered confectionery sugar, ½ teaspoon of vanilla extract, 1 cup of whipping cream, crushed ice, 1 cup of rock salt, and a spoon. The children should pour all of the liquid ingredients plus the sugar into the smaller bag, seal it, and shake to mix. Next, they should place the smaller bag inside the bigger one, scoop in as much ice as the big bag can hold but still close, then sprinkle in rock salt. After sealing the big bag, the children will need to wear oven mitts to hold and shake the bag. The bag should be shaken until the liquid feels thick when the bag is squeezed gently.

CHAPTER 3

Physics in the Kitchen

Stack a Drink ②

Investigate how to make a liquid more dense or thick. Then use what you discover to assemble a colorful and tasty layered drink.

FUEL UP

measuring cup
1 cup grape juice
3 juice glasses
1 tablespoon sugar
spoon
½ cup orange juice
water
¼ cup apple juice
tall 12-ounce (350-ml) water glass
straw

BLAST OFF!

1. Pour the cup of grape juice into one of the juice glasses. Add the sugar and stir with the spoon until the crystals dissolve and disappear.

2. Pour the orange juice into another juice glass. Add 1 cup of water and stir.

3. Pour the apple juice into the third juice glass. Add ¾ cup of water and stir.

4. Pour enough of the grape juice into the water glass to fill it about a third full.

5. Slowly spoon orange juice on top of the grape juice. Let the juice slip off the spoon.

6. Slowly spoon the apple juice on top of the orange juice.

7. View your stacked juice drink from the side to see the layers. Then slowly insert the straw. Try sipping one layer at a time.

Brain Booster

There was a little mixing where the layers touched, but as long as the glass was kept still, the layers of juice stayed stacked. That's because the more sugary and less watery juices are denser, or thicker, than the others. Juices that are less dense will float on those that are denser. If you choose not to drink the juice, you can watch what happens later. Over time, **diffusion**, the process of something spreading out from where there is a lot of it to where there is very little, will cause the liquids to mix. Find out how long it takes for diffusion to make the different colored juices mix.

Bonus Pack

Drop a hard-boiled egg into a glass of water, and it will sink to the bottom. But with a little trial and error, you can add just enough salt to the water to make the egg float in the middle of the glass. Each time you add more salt, first remove the egg from the water with a spoon. Mix in about a teaspoonful of salt and stir well to dissolve it. Then use the spoon to slip the egg back into the water.

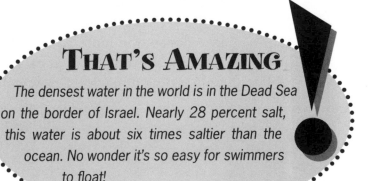

That's Amazing

The densest water in the world is in the Dead Sea on the border of Israel. Nearly 28 percent salt, this water is about six times saltier than the ocean. No wonder it's so easy for swimmers to float!

Always Pick the Winner ③

Investigate how the density of a substance affects the way it moves—even the amount of energy that it uses to roll downhill.

Fuel Up

3-foot (0.9-m) square board
cereal box
can of condensed chicken noodle soup
can of condensed tomato soup
Note: Pick soups that are the same brand and cans that are identical except for their contents.

Blast Off!

1. Work on a smooth, flat floor.

2. Prop up one end of the board on the cereal box.

3. At the raised end of the board, line up the two cans—curved side down and side by side.

4. Release both cans at the same instant. Which can wins?

5. Repeat the race several times to be sure the results are likely to happen every time.

Brain Booster

The can of chicken noodle soup was the winner. This happened because even though both cans contained condensed soups, meaning that most of the water had been removed from the liquid, the chicken noodle was less dense and more liquid. At the start of the race, both soups had exactly the same amount of potential energy—the energy that was available for the cans to roll downhill. As the cans rolled, the contents swirled around inside. The less dense chicken noodle soup just flowed downhill, so most of its potential energy was used to propel the can forward. The denser tomato soup, however, used up part of its potential energy to make the thick condensed soup turn around inside the rolling can, so it had less energy left to propel the can forward.

Bonus Pack

Find out what happens when other kinds of soups race. Always think about which can contains the most liquid soup before the race starts, and you're likely to pick the winner. Which kind of soup beats all of the rest?

Make a Boomerang Can ②

Investigate how to store up energy. Then discover how energy can produce a fun activity.

Fuel Up

can opener

2 identical empty 1-pound (0.45-kg), or larger, metal cans, such as coffee cans, with plastic snap-on lids

scissors

elastic strip 2 inches (5 cm) longer than the can (available at stores that sell sewing supplies)

2 darning needles (available at stores that sell knitting supplies)

3 metal washers (available at hardware stores)

metal twist tie, such as a bread-bag tie

Blast Off!

1. Use the can opener to remove the bottom from one of the cans. You won't need the second can—only its lid.

2. Use the scissors to cut a slit in the center of each plastic lid. Make the slit slightly longer than the width of the elastic strip.

3. Push one end of the elastic strip through the slit in one of plastic lids from the inside to the outside. Have an adult stick the darning needle through the strip to keep it from slipping back through the lid.

4. Slide the can over the elastic strip and snap on the lid.

5. Thread the washers onto the middle of the twist tie.

6. Tie the washers to the center of the elastic strip.

7. Thread the remaining end of the elastic strip—from the inside to the outside—through the other plastic lid.

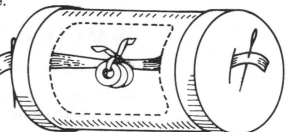

8. Snap the lid on the can, pulling the elastic strip tight.

9. Anchor the elastic strip with the other needle.

10. On a smooth flat floor, gently push the can to roll it away from you.

Brain Booster

The can rolled forward until it slowed so much that it nearly stopped. Then it rolled back again. This happened because the sections of the elastic strip that were closest to the lids turned with the can, but the weighted center didn't. So the elastic band became wound up while the can rolled away from you. When the can slowed down, the elastic band started to unwind. That made the can roll back to you.

Bonus Pack

See how far you can get the can to roll away and still return. Test to find out if putting a heavier weight on the center of the elastic band increases how far the can will roll away and return.

Bend a Spoon without Touching It ①

This hands-on activity is perfect for first-time science explorers. First, play flashlight tag in a dimly lit room to let kids discover that light usually travels in a straight line. Next, let them conduct this easy experiment to see how the path of light bends when it passes from air through another kind of matter and back through air. The result is an easy-to-see optical illusion that will make this activity memorable.

Fuel Up

tall 12-ounce (350-ml) water glass
water
long-handled spoon

Blast Off!

1. Fill the glass two-thirds full of water.

2. Place the spoon—with the bowl end down—in the glass, resting the handle against the side.

3. Look at the spoon through the side of the glass.

BRAIN BOOSTER

Light usually travels in a straight line, but when light passes from matter with one kind of density into matter of a different density, the light waves change direction. This shift is called **refraction**. In this activity, the light waves were bent as they traveled both into and back out of the water. That bending made the part of the spoon below the surface of the water appear to be slightly to one side of the handle above the surface.

BONUS PACK

If you have a prism available, use a flashlight to shine a beam of light through it, creating a rainbow-colored light beam. Visible light is actually made up of different colors of light all traveling together. But when a beam of light is refracted, each color of light is slowed to a slightly different rate in comparison with the others. The colored lights separate into a spectrum of red, orange, yellow, green, blue, indigo, and violet. Raindrops are nature's prisms. On a warm, sunny day, go outdoors and let your youngsters use a hose to spray a mist of water into the air. As the water drops bend the light rays, kids will see a spectrum in the form of a rainbow.

Or indoors, you can place a flat mirror against the inside of a glass bowl full of water. Have a partner shine a bright flashlight through the bowl so that the beam strikes the mirror. Move a white piece of paper around outside the bowl until a rainbow of colors appears on it. The water between the mirror and the water's surface in the bowl acts like a prism to split up the light ray into colors.

Make a Coin Appear ②

Use refraction to create another fun optical illusion.

FUEL UP

> penny
> shallow cereal bowl
> water

BLAST OFF!

1. Place the penny in the bottom of the cereal bowl.
2. Set the bowl on the kitchen counter.

THAT'S AMAZING

To catch **prey**, the living things caught by predators, the archerfish of Southeast Asia spits a jet of water at insects that hang on leaves and branches above the pool, in order to knock the insects into the water. In spite of refraction making the insects appear to be somewhere they're not, the fish usually hits its target—even at a distance greater than 4 feet (1.2 m).

3. Bend down so that the rim of the bowl is even with your nose, and you're unable to see the coin.

4. While you watch, have a partner pour water into the bowl.

BRAIN BOOSTER

As water was poured into the bowl, the coin became visible. Refraction of the light bouncing off the coin made an image of the coin appear above the actual coin. That's what you saw.

BONUS PACK

When the water is poured into the bowl and you first see the coin, try to touch what you see. Because refraction makes the image of the coin appear above the real coin, your finger will touch only water.

Put a Balloon in a Candle Flame ①

This activity is a dramatic demonstration of one way to transfer heat energy.

FUEL UP

water
a round balloon
a candle in a holder
oven mitt
matches (for adult use only)

BLAST OFF!

1. Pour ¼ cup of water into the balloon.

2. Blow into the balloon to inflate it and tie the neck of the balloon to seal it.

3. Set the candle in the kitchen sink and have an adult light it.

4. Have an adult wearing an oven mitt hold the balloon by its tied neck and lower it until the fattest end of the balloon touches the flame.

Brain Booster

The balloon didn't pop. A balloon's rubber skin is thin and fragile. Usually, a flame will make the spot it touches hot enough that the rubber will melt and the balloon will pop. But water is an excellent conductor of heat, and in this project, it drew heat from the spot that was heated by the flame.

Bonus Pack

Use what you discovered to make hot chocolate in a paper cup. With a hole punch, make a hole just below the cup's rim. Make a second hole opposite the first one. Tie on a string handle. Fill the cup half full of water. Loop the handle over the bowl end of a long wooden spoon. Set a candle in the kitchen sink, have an adult light it, and hold the paper cup in the flame. Like the rubber balloon, the cup won't burn because water is drawing heat away from the paper. You may need to take turns holding the cup, as the water will take a few minutes to boil. When it does, remove it from the flame and immediately stir in a tablespoon of hot chocolate mix. Let the drink cool a bit and enjoy.

Separate Pepper from Salt ①

There's more than one way to accomplish this challenge. For the youngest investigators, this project is a perfect introduction to **static electricity**, electrons or charged bits that collect in one place, instead of flowing from one place to another.

Fuel Up

rubber balloon
2 tablespoons coarse pepper flakes (available at grocery stores)
2 tablespoons table salt
2 plates
spoon

BLAST OFF!

1. Blow up the balloon and tie the neck to seal it.

2. Pour the pepper and salt on one of the plates and stir with a spoon to mix well.

3. Rub the balloon briskly against your hair (or against a wool sweater).

4. Touch the balloon to the surface of the pepper and salt mixture.

5. Brush any pepper flakes that stick to the balloon onto the empty plate.

6. Repeat rubbing and touching the balloon to the pepper and salt mixture until no more pepper flakes collect on the balloon.

BRAIN BOOSTER

You were able to use static electricity to attract the pepper flakes. Electricity comes from charged particles in matter called **electrons**. Electrons are normally parts of atoms, the building blocks of molecules. Sometimes, though, electrons are knocked out of their atoms. Then those free electrons may be collected in one place or may move from one place to another. When the electrons collect in one place, the charged bits are called static electricity. Rubbing the balloon on hair or wool knocked some electrons free, and they collected on the balloon's surface. When this weak charge was brought close to the plate, the pepper and the salt became charged, too. Because the pepper and salt mixture and the balloon were charged differently, the two unlike charges attracted each other. And, because the pepper was so light, that pull was enough to lift the lightest flakes. This method isn't a complete success, though. Some of the tiniest, lightest bits of salt are also likely to be attracted and to stick to the balloon, and heavier pieces of pepper won't be lifted by the charge in the balloon.

Another Way to Separate Pepper from Salt ②

Let older children brainstorm ways to separate pepper from a mixture of salt and pepper. They could start with the static electricity activity and then think of other strategies. The following technique relies on the fact that salt, like many other solids, dissolves in water.

FUEL UP

2 tablespoons coarse pepper flakes (available at grocery stores)
2 tablespoons table salt
glass pie plate
water
spoon
piece of old nylon stocking or cotton cloth
rubber band
tall 12-ounce (350-ml) water glass

BLAST OFF!

1. Pour the pepper and salt into the pie plate.

2. Add a cup of water and stir with the spoon until the salt grains are no longer visible.

3. Cover the glass with the cloth and secure with the rubber band.

4. Pour the solution from the pie plate into the water glass.

BRAIN BOOSTER

The pepper flakes were left on the cloth. The salt seemed to have disappeared. In fact, the salt grains have dissolved, meaning they've broken down and become suspended in the water.

BONUS PACK

Prove that the salt is in the water. Pour the water from the glass back into the pie plate. Let it set until the water has evaporated (moved into the air). This will take a couple of days, but after it happens, only the salt will remain. It will be a crusty layer coating the bottom of the pie plate. This is similar to the method that's used to extract salt from seawater.

Cut Ice with Wire ②

Find out how pressure affects ice.

FUEL UP

3 paper cups
2-liter empty plastic drink bottle, with a flat-topped cap
water

cork drink coaster
paper towel folded into fourths
18-inch (45-cm) piece of strong, thin wire
2 sturdy coffee mugs with handles (Be sure you have an adult's permission to use these.)

Blast Off!

1. Fill one paper cup half full of water and freeze.

2. Fill the drink bottle full of water to give it weight, put on the cap, and set the bottle in the kitchen sink.

3. Place the coaster on top of the bottle and cover it with the folded paper towel.

4. Peel the paper cup off the ice and set the ice block on top of the paper towel.

5. Twist one end of the wire around the handle of each coffee mug.

6. Place the wire across the middle of the ice block. If necessary, shorten the wire so that both coffee cups are suspended in the air.

7. Check the ice block every 15 minutes.

Brain Booster

The ice melted where the wire touched it. That happened because the weight of the coffee mugs put pressure on the wire. The pressure caused the ice to heat up and melt beneath the wire. If you use something heavier than coffee mugs or carefully add coins or other weights to the tipped cups, it will increase the pressure and make the wire slice through the ice faster. This is the same thing that happens when someone ice skates. The person's body weight puts pressure on the skate blades. This makes the ice melt under the blades, and the skater actually slides along on this slick, melted surface.

Bonus Pack

Obtain a piece of dry ice; it's usually available through stores that carry party supplies or from an ice supplier. (*Caution: Use dry ice only with an adult's supervision. Never touch dry ice with your bare hands.*) Dry ice is frozen carbon dioxide gas, rather than water, but it also melts under pressure. Be sure to wear oven mitts for this experiment; then press a metal spoon against the ice. The melting dry ice releases carbon dioxide gas. As the gas slips from under the spoon, it causes the metal to vibrate just enough to make a screamlike noise.

For More Science in the Kitchen Fun

Emeril's There's a Chef in My Soup! Recipes for the Kid in Everyone by Emeril Lagasse (New York: HarperCollins, 2002). Packed with 75 fun, tasty recipes with easy-to-follow instructions. Ages 9–12.

Everything Kids' Cookbook: From Mac 'n' Cheese to Double Chocolate Chip Cookies—All You Need to Have Some Finger Lickin' Fun by Sandra Nissenberg (Avon, Mass.: Adams Media Corporation, 2002). Trivia, puzzles, cooking tips, and recipes for tasty and healthful food. This is a book that kids and parents can enjoy together. Ages 9–12.

Grow Your Own Pizza: Gardening Plans and Recipes for Kids by Constance Hardesty (Golden, Colo.: Fulcrum Publishers, 2003). Recipes and activities for blossoming gardeners and chefs. Ages 9–12.

How to Read a French Fry: And Other Stories of Intriguing Kitchen Science by Russ Parsons (New York: Houghton Mifflin Company, 2003). This book includes recipes, the science behind the recipes, and food lore. It also includes valuable explanations such as what makes apples "mealy." Ages 9–12.

Pretend Soup and Other Real Recipes: A Cookbook for Preschoolers and Up by Mollie Katzen and Ann L. Henderson (Berkeley, Calif.: Tricycle Press, 1994). Easy-to-follow illustrated recipes for adults to share with children. Ages 4–8.

Science Experiments You Can Eat, revised edition, by Vicki Cobb (New York: Harper Trophy, 1994). This book has plenty of action for the kitchen laboratory and budding scientists. Ages 7 and up.

The Science Chef: 100 Fun Food Experiments and Recipes for Kids by Joan D'Amico (New York: John Wiley & Sons, 1994). This book reveals what happens to change ingredients into food. There's plenty of fascinating trivia, too. Ages 9–12.

The Secret Life of Food by Clare Crespo (New York: Hyperion Press, 2002). Quirky and amazingly simple recipes for making everything from sushi cupcakes to chocolate cake baked in terra-cotta pots. This is a culinary adventure. Ages 9–12.

PART
II
Science in the Backyard

. . . .

Grow a living playroom in the garden. Make a heart appear on a leaf. Make your own colored chalk to create sidewalk art. Race boats powered by a chemical reaction. Build a catapult to launch jellybeans at a target. And lots more! The backyard is a great place for science discovery fun.

. . . .

CHAPTER 4

Biology in the Backyard

Test an Ant's IQ ②

Observe how ants behave as they tackle the challenges you set up for them.

FUEL UP

1 tablespoon granulated sugar in a self-sealing plastic bag
5 toothpicks
1 tablespoon water in a self-sealing plastic bag
5 raisins in a self-sealing plastic bag

BLAST OFF!

1. Find ants that are crawling across a sidewalk.

2. Place a few grains of sugar a little ways ahead and to the left of the ants. Do the ants find the sugar? How do they react?

3. Place a toothpick in the path of the ants. How do they react when they first come to the toothpick? How do they overcome this obstacle?

4. Drip water to form a U-shaped barrier in the ants' path. How do they react when they first encounter this obstacle? How do they overcome it?

5. Scatter the raisins in front of and behind the traveling ants. Do the ants find all of the raisins? How do they react?

6. Think up other challenges for the ants. Because some ants sting, check with an adult to make sure that each test will be safe. Then try it.

Brain Booster

Ants use their antennae, the long projections from their heads, to smell, touch, and taste. Ants spend a lot of time searching for food. As they travel, they lay down a scent trail they can follow back to their nest. Some ants also observe "landmarks" and use these to make a fast, direct trip home once they find food. You probably noticed that ants appear to follow each other in a line, even when it is a winding path around obstacles. Ants communicate with each other by releasing odors and by vibrating their bodies. Then other ants are able to detect these odors and vibrations with their antennae.

Bonus Pack

Create a mini–obstacle course outdoors, then time how quickly each person can complete its challenges. Choose a flat open area. To outline a curving path, use milk jugs, soft drink bottles, or even paper lunch sacks partly filled with sand. Add fun obstacles, including a 2-by-4 board to walk along, paired circles of yarn to hop through, a yardstick stretched between two chairs to crawl under, and stuffed animals to hop over. Create especially challenging events along the course, such as a tunnel to crawl through. This could be a box with the bottom and the top removed or a table topped with a blanket. You could also create a swamp for kids to crawl across. To create the swamp, pile up old blankets and old pillows or use an inflated mattress.

Build an Ant Farm ②

Investigate how ants build their home in the ground by giving them a home that's easy to observe.

FUEL UP

half-gallon (2-l) clear plastic bottle with screw-on cap

scissors

pint-sized (473-ml) plastic jar with screw-on lid

measuring cup

potting soil

cardboard box—large enough for baking tray to easily fit in the bottom

duct tape

disposable aluminum baking tray

2 cups water

*1 tablespoon sugar

*1 cup warm water

*12 cotton balls (10 are used to capture ants—see Ant Hunting Tips; 2 are used in the Ant Care Guide)

*2 self-sealing plastic sandwich bags

*cooking oil

*sturdy paper or plastic cup

*rubber gloves or rubber gardening gloves

*clear plastic wrap

*rubber band

*funnel

*3 to 4 teaspoons bread crumbs (these are used in the Ant Care Guide)

BLAST OFF!

1. Cut the top off the plastic bottle just below the neck.

2. Have an adult use the scissors to poke several holes in the top section of the bottle.

3. Screw the lid on the jar and set it in the middle of the bottom of the plastic bottle. This takes up space in the middle of the ant farm and will force the ants to build their tunnels close to the sides of the bottle, where you can easily see them.

4. Using a measuring cup, scoop potting soil into the bottom of the plastic bottle until it fills the area around the jar.

5. On the cardboard box, cut and fold down a flap almost as large as one side of the box.

6. Put the top of the plastic bottle back onto the bottle's bottom and seal with duct tape.

7. Read the Ant Hunting Tips on this page and collect at least a dozen ants from the same group of ants.

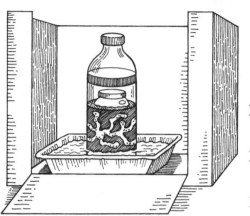

8. Set the box in a warm place indoors that is out of the sun.

9. Place the aluminum tray inside the box. Set the bottle in the middle of the tray. Pour 2 cups of water into the tray to trap any ants that escape the bottle.

10. Add the ants to the colony through the top of the plastic bottle. Screw on the cap.

11. Follow the steps in the Ant Care Guide on page 59 and add food and water as needed.

12. At least once a day, fold down the viewing flap and watch the ants in your colony.

Ant Hunting Tips

If you live in an area where certain varieties of ants, such as fire ants, cause painful stings, it's best to avoid them and purchase your ants from a local pet supply center or online. Ants are usually inexpensive and travel well.

If the ants in your area aren't the stinging or biting kind, and if you want to collect your own, start by preparing a lure. Stir 1 tablespoon of sugar into a cup of warm water until it dissolves. Soak 10 cotton balls in this sugar water, then place them in a self-sealing plastic sandwich bag. Rub cooking oil around the rim of a sturdy paper or plastic cup, and place this in another self-sealing plastic bag.

Go outdoors to look for an anthill. Place the cotton balls around the anthill to help draw the ants up. Then let an adult who is wearing rubber gloves or rubber gardening gloves scoop up the ants with the cup. Using this method, you will undoubtedly collect only workers, and that is sufficient for your purpose of observing ants in action underground. It also won't have a major impact on the ant colony.

The oil will be a climbing barrier for the ants, but the adult still must work quickly to top the cup with clear plastic wrap and seal it with a rubber band. Then the cup of ants can be returned to the self-sealing plastic bag.

At home, place the bag of ants in the refrigerator for 10 minutes. Cooling will slow them down. Then an adult who is wearing rubber gloves can remove the plastic wrap and pour the ants through a funnel into their new home.

13. For 2 weeks, keep a journal of what the ants are doing and include sketches of their tunneling efforts.

14. When you are done observing the ants, ask an adult who is wearing rubber gloves to take the ant farm outdoors, remove the duct tape, and dump out the colony close to where the ants were collected.

Brain Booster

A typical ant colony is made up mainly of workers, with one or more queens and developing young. The workers build the nest, guard it, carry home food, and care for the young. The queen starts the colony and maintains it by laying eggs that develop into young workers. Like all insects, ants have six legs. They also have antennae that give them their senses of touch and taste. Ants have strong jaws but can't chew. Their food is mainly the juice they squeeze from bits of food. Worker ants can live from 45 to 60 days. Some queens live for years.

Ant Care Guide

Soak a cotton ball in water and squeeze lightly. Unscrew the bottle cap and drop this into the colony. Every 2 days, drop in a pinch (about ¼ teaspoon) of bread crumbs. At the end of the first week, drop in a second wet cotton ball. Don't worry about removing the first one.

Bonus Pack

In certain parts of the world, people eat ants as well as other insects. In Japan, some people eat boiled wasp larvae and fried cicadas. In Nigeria, the menu might include roasted termites; in Bali, supper could be barbecued dragonfly; and in New Zealand, the native Maoris enjoy huhu (pronounced who-who) larvae. People who eat ants report that these insects have a vinegary taste. Rather than serving up the real thing, let your family dine on this healthful fake ant snack. Wash and slice celery sticks into logs. Spread cream cheese on each log and stick on a line of raisin ants.

That's Amazing

Ants are super-strong for their size. A person as strong as an ant wouldn't have any trouble carrying a small car up to the top of Mount Everest. Some ants carry objects weighing fifty times more than they do over long distances and even up tall trees.

Make a Bug Catcher ①

Any walk can be a nature hunt when you take time to look around. Make this junior bug-hunting tool to help young explorers enjoy their first expeditions.

FUEL UP

scissors
sturdy paper plate
old panty hose
duct tape
paint-stirring stick

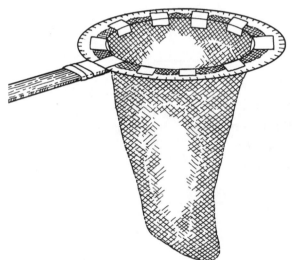

BLAST OFF!

1. Use scissors to cut the center out of a paper plate.
2. Cut one leg off the panty hose. Put this through the plate ring and tape the cloth to the edges.
3. Use more tape to attach the paint-stirring stick as a handle for the net.
4. Catch butterflies and other bugs with the net. Observe and release them.

BRAIN BOOSTER

In addition to seeing animals, you likely found evidence that animals were in your backyard. For example, you may have discovered chewed leaves that caterpillars munched, as well as galls, bumps on plants where insect larvae, or young, developed. You might also have found a web that a spider built, nutshells left by a squirrel, and footprints left by a mouse or another animal. Besides flowers and other plants that your family planted, you likely discovered wild plants, also called weeds.

BONUS PACK

Turn the duct tape sticky side out and make a loop big enough to wear as a bracelet. Collect flowers, seeds, leaves, feathers, and more to stick onto this "wild" bracelet.

Go on a Night Safari ③

Exploring your backyard at night will let young investigators discover creatures that are usually active only after dark.

FUEL UP

one flashlight per person

garden trowel

plastic pint-sized (473-ml) jar with screw-on lid

1 tablespoon ground beef in a self-sealing plastic bag

plastic picnic plate

a rock and a pebble

strip of cloth

paint brush

bait mix: either 3 bananas, ¼ cup water, and 1 tablespoon sugar; or 1 cup creamy peanut butter and 3 tablespoons vegetable oil; or 1 cup cornstarch and a 12-ounce (350-ml) can of beer

6-volt lantern

white sheet

BLAST OFF!

1. Go hunting for slugs and snails. To find them, use the flashlight to discover silvery trails across paved areas. These are paths of slippery mucouslike material the slugs and snails deposited to make it easier for them to slip across the surface.

2. Build a Beetle Trap. To do this, use the garden trowel to dig a hole in the ground just big enough for your jar. Drop in the bit of ground beef. Cover the jar with the plastic plate. Weigh this down with a rock. Then prop up one corner with a pebble. Do this the night before your safari.

3. Build a Bait Trap. Do this during the day before your nighttime safari so that it's ready to attract insects. First, tie a strip of cloth around a tree's trunk so that you can easily find the tree at night. Then use a brush to paint one of the following mixtures on the **bark**, the outer protective covering of the tree, just below the knot in the cloth. Fruit Mix: Mash up 3 ripe bananas. Stir in ¼ cup of water and 1 tablespoon of sugar. Peanut Butter Mix: Mix together 1 cup of creamy peanut butter and 3 tablespoons of vegetable oil. Beer Mix: Stir 1 cup of cornstarch into a 12-ounce (350-ml) can of beer.

4. Build a Light Trap. Switch on the lantern and cover it with the white sheet. Wait quietly to see what arrives and lands on the sheet.

BRAIN BOOSTER

The difference between slugs and snails is that snails have shells. If you found a slug or a snail, you probably noticed the big muscular "foot" that ran the length of its body. These animals propel themselves along by sending waves of contractions from the back to the front of this foot. To help themselves slide easily across dry surfaces, they give off a mucouslike material that's similar to the stuff that comes out of your nose. Snails and slugs slide along on this slippery stuff.

There are more than 300,000 different kinds of beetles, so the types you found depended on which ones live in your area. Beetles are known for having hard coverings over their wings. Adults have big jaws called mandibles to chew plants or eat other insects. Some that you might have seen are ladybugs and Japanese beetles.

The Bait Trap and the Light Trap probably attracted all sorts of flying insects. Moths were the stars of the show, and, again, what kind you saw depended on where you live. This is a good time, though, to notice the features that characterize a moth. Look for

- feathery antennae (butterflies have knobbed ends on their antennae),

- wings spread out horizontally when at rest (butterflies hold their wings up, vertically above their bodies when at rest),

- hairy bodies (butterflies are much less hairy).

BONUS PACK

If fireflies live in your area, try to communicate with them. Go outdoors on a warm, clear night and take along a flashlight. Sit quietly and watch fireflies flashing around you. The male and female fireflies flash in order to find each other. The males fly, while the females usually stay perched on a blade of grass. You'll see that these flashing patterns range from single short flashes to long flashes. Try mimicking one of the patterns you observe to see if you attract any fireflies.

Just so you know, fireflies are not flies. They are related to beetles. The adults usually feed on nectar, the sweet juice produced by plants. Firefly larvae (young) usually eat snails and slugs. Fireflies are able to produce light through a process called bioluminescence. This is a chemical reaction that happens when luciferin, a protein manufactured in a firefly's body, is acted on and broken down with the help of luciferase, a kind of enzyme. By the way, during the process of producing light, bioluminescence gives off almost no heat.

Get a Sip from a Plant ③

Plants need to take in water through their roots to stay alive, but they also give off water through other parts. This activity will let you taste how this happens.

Fuel Up

leafy potted plant, such as a geranium
large, clean kitchen bag, such as an unused trash bag
string
a clean straw

Blast Off!

1. Set the plant inside the bag.
2. Pull the bag up enough to completely surround the plant.
3. Twist the open end of the bag to seal it, then secure this with the string.
4. Place the bagged plant in a warm place but not in direct sunlight.
5. Wait an hour. Then open the bag and use the straw to sip some of the water drops that collected on the inside of the bag.

Brain Booster

The plant gave off water through tiny openings in its leaves. In a green plant, a process called capillary action (in which water moves up into the plant) begins when water in the leaves evaporates or changes from a liquid to a gas—**water vapor**. This creates spaces between the molecules of the leaf's tissue. Water that's already in the leaf stem moves into these spaces, and more water molecules move in behind. This process continues all the way down to the roots, where fresh water molecules are pulled in from the soil.

Most of the water that evaporated from the plant was in the air trapped inside the bag. When the air came in contact with the plastic, it cooled a little—enough to cause **condensation**, the process of water vapor changing to a liquid as the molecules slowed down.

BONUS PACK

Prove that the water really escapes from leaves. Start with two green leaves that you've removed from a plant or a tree. Spread petroleum jelly over the upper and lower surfaces of one leaf. Set the two leaves side by side in a warm but not sunny spot. Wait a day, then check both leaves. The uncoated leaf will feel much stiffer and may even be brittle because the water inside the leaf will have escaped, without being replaced. The petroleum jelly–coated leaf won't lose as much water because the petroleum jelly will plug up the holes in the leaves that allow the water to escape, so the leaf will still be flexible.

THAT'S AMAZING

About 60 percent of a plant's weight is water, so it's no wonder that a large tree loses many gallons of water on a warm, sunny day. Can you guess why a pine tree is likely to lose less than an oak does? Its needlelike leaves have less surface area from which water can escape.

Grow a Room ③

Plant sunflowers and observe how they grow. Once the plants are in bloom, you can enjoy a unique living room.

FUEL UP

sunny garden area with loose, free-draining soil
paper towels
spray bottle of water
sturdy paper plate
2 packages sunflower seeds—or about 50 seeds—of one of the tallest varieties: Cyclops Hybrid, Giant Yellow, Giganteus, Kong Hybrid, Mammoth Russian, or Sunzilla
general flower fertilizer

BLAST OFF!

1. After there isn't any chance of frost in your area, soak a paper towel with water, squeeze out the excess, and place it on the paper plate.

2. Place the seeds on the wet towel, making sure that none of them overlap.

3. Wet and squeeze out a second paper towel. Cover the seeds with the wet towel.

4. Use the spray bottle to mist the paper towel with water every day.

5. In about a week, the seeds that are going to grow will have sprouted. Plant these in a circle in the outdoor area you've chosen, placing the seeds just beneath the surface, about 12 inches (30 cm) apart.

6. Keep the plants watered. Fertilize about a week after the seeds are planted and every week until the flowers have fully developed. The sunflowers will grow to their full height and will flower in about 3 months. If necessary, stake the plants as the flowers develop.

7. Sit inside the circle of sunflower plants to watch these giants grow, and observe their behavior once the flowers begin to develop. When the flowers are full grown, enjoy some private time in this *living* room. Toss down some old pillows, kick back, and read a book, such as *Sunflower House* by Eve Bunting (San Diego, Calif.: Voyager Books, 1999). Or bring paints or crayons and paper to create a picture of the sunflowers.

Brain Booster

Plants grow toward where they can get the most exposure to sunlight. This process is called **phototropism**, which means "moving toward light." Since a plant can't pull up its roots and relocate, one side of its stem—the side that receives less light exposure—grows faster than the other. This makes the plant's stem bend so that the rest of the plant gets closer to the light source. In young sunflowers, the stems grow in a way that makes the developing flowers track the sun from east to west during the day. However, as the flowers develop, the stems become woodier to support the heavy blooms. Then the flowers usually become locked, facing east. While no one knows for sure, it's possible that this keeps the flower from being exposed to the sun during the hottest part of the day.

Bonus Pack

Harvest the flower heads once the back surface has turned very dark. Each sunflower will have hundreds of seeds. Dry these and put some out for the birds, but also roast some for yourself.

Spread the seeds in a metal cake pan. Place the pan in a 300°F (148°C) oven for about 30 minutes or until golden brown. Ask an adult wearing oven mitts to take the pan out of the oven; then mix the seeds in a bowl with 1 tablespoon of margarine or butter while the seeds are still hot. Scoop them onto waxed paper and sprinkle with salt. When the seeds are cool, they're ready to munch. After you start to chew, you'll want to spit out the hulls; then you can enjoy the nutty kernels.

Make a Heart Appear on a Leaf ③

Kids will discover why leaves change color, as they use this process to decorate a plant's leaves.

FUEL UP

scissors
3-by-5-inch (7.5-by-12.5-cm) piece of construction paper
potted geranium
masking tape

BLAST OFF!

1. Using scissors, cut a heart shape out of the paper. Trim it to a size that's a little smaller than one of the plant's largest leaves.

2. Make a loop of tape and stick it to one side of the heart.

3. Use tape to stick the heart to the upper surface of the leaf.

4. Place the plant in a sunny location and wait for 5 days.

5. Remove the paper to reveal the pale heart shape underneath.

BRAIN BOOSTER

The pale heart shape appeared where light was blocked from reaching the leaf. When exposed to sunlight, a green plant's leaves are food factories. Through a process called **photosynthesis**, chlorophyll molecules in the plant's tissues, especially in its leaves, absorb light energy from the sun and use it to change **carbon dioxide** gas (the gas in the air that the plants need for this process) and water into sugar and a waste gas, oxygen. The plant's leaves look green because of all the chlorophyll they contain. The chlorophyll quickly breaks down, but as long as the tissues are exposed to sunlight, they keep on producing more chlorophyll.

Putting paper over part of the leaf kept that area from being exposed to sunlight, so, in that area, chlorophyll production stopped. Plant leaves contain other coloring pigments, such as carotene, which appears yellow. Chlorophyll usually masks any other coloring matter, but when chlorophyll production stops, the other colors are exposed. The same thing happens on a large scale when, during autumn, the days grow shorter. In some trees, hidden pigments, like carotene, are revealed when chlorophyll production stops. That's why birches, aspens, and cottonwoods look golden in fall. In other trees, sugar is trapped in the leaves, causing a chemical reaction that produces a red pigment. That's what happens to make maple leaves appear red.

THAT'S AMAZING

In ancient times, Native Americans told stories to explain why things happened. They explained that the leaves turned color when the hunters in the sky killed the Great Bear, the name given to the constellation that's also called the Big Dipper. The Great Bear's blood poured down, coloring some of the trees of the forests red. Then as the hunters cooked the Great Bear, the fat splashed out of the kettle and rained down, coloring other trees yellow.

Be a Bird Detective ③

Work together to assemble a "tweet treat" buffet to attract birds. Check the Brain Booster on page 69 to see what food to offer common varieties of birds.

FUEL UP

For Tweet Treat 1:
  18-inch (45-cm) piece of sturdy string or twine
  stale bagel
  mixing bowl
  spoon
  3 tablespoons yellow cornmeal
  ¼ cup raisins
  1 cup crunchy peanut butter

For Tweet Treat 2:
  2 cups red milo
  2 cups black oil sunflower seeds
  2 cups cracked corn

BLAST OFF!

1. Build Tweet Treat 1.

- Tie the ends of the string together. Lay the bagel on the string loop. Thread the knotted end through this loop and pull tight.

- Mix together the cornmeal, raisins, and peanut butter.

- Spread the mixture on the bagel.

- Hang the bagel in a tree where it's easy to watch.

2. Build Tweet Treat 2.

- Find a clear, open area that's easy to watch.

- Pour out separate piles of each kind of seed.

3. Keep a list of what kinds of birds come to eat at each of your feeders. Use bird books to help you identify those you don't know.

4. Add more food as it's needed and observe the birds to discover the following:

- What time of day do the birds most often show up to eat—morning, afternoon, or evening?

- Do the birds usually feed one at a time or in groups?

- Do the same birds that eat on the ground also eat from the hanging feeders?
- Do some birds chase away others?
- What other animals, such as squirrels and chipmunks, come to eat?

BRAIN BOOSTER

Just like people, birds have favorite kinds of food and preferred places to dine. Some, like sparrows and mourning doves, prefer seeds and like to eat on the ground. Others, like chickadees and finches, eat seeds but prefer to perch above the ground. Still others, like robins and woodpeckers, commonly eat insects. Those are the ones that will delight in nibbling the peanut butter and raisins. What type of birds you see will also depend on those that are in your area at different times of the year.

If you live in North America, you may want to participate in a continent-wide study of what birds like to eat. Contact Project Feeder Watch in the United States (Cornell Lab of Ornithology, 159 Sapsucker Woods Road, Ithaca, NY 14850) or in Canada (Long Point Bird Observatory, Post Office Box 160, Port Rowan, Ontario, Canada N0E 1M0). Or check for information online at http://birds.cornell.edu/pfw/.

BONUS PACK

Your family could plant trees and shrubs that will provide food, shelter, and nesting places for birds. You'll need to check with your local nursery to see which types will likely grow well in your area, but here are some to consider. Ash trees, barberries, chokeberries, elms, junipers, roses, and wax myrtles supply fruit or berries. Pines, spicebushes, magnolias, and beech trees supply seeds or nuts. Hibiscus, mimosas, tulip trees, and wigelia supply nectar.

You may want to turn your backyard into a wildlife **habitat**, the place in the world that provides the things animals need to live. The National Wildlife Federation supplies information on how you can be sure that your backyard provides water, food, and shelter for wildlife. Whether it's big or as tiny as a balcony, you can still provide what's needed and get your backyard officially registered as a wildlife habitat. Then you'll receive a certificate, and your backyard will be entered into the National Registry of Backyard Wildlife Habitats. For more information, check online at www.nwf.org/backyardwildlifehabitat/ or write to National Wildlife Federation, Backyard Wildlife Habitat Questions, 11100 Wildlife Center Drive, Reston, VA 20190-5362.

CHAPTER 5
Chemistry in the Backyard

Lighten Up a T-Shirt ②

Bleaching is the process of removing the natural color of cloth, paper, or even hair. In this case, bleaching is also a chance to be creative with a reverse tie-dying project.

FUEL UP

outdoor area
2 plastic buckets
measuring cup
water
liquid laundry bleach (for adult use only)
dark blue, red, or other dark-colored cotton T-shirt
6 rubber bands
rubber gloves

BLAST OFF!

1. Do this activity outdoors on a sunny day. Wear old clothes and try not to splash the bleach or bleach water on them.

2. Fill 1 bucket two-thirds full of water. Have an adult pour 2 cups of laundry bleach into the second bucket. Add 4 cups of water.

3. Gather up a handful of cloth from the front of the T-shirt and twist it. Wrap a rubber band tightly around the twisted cloth to secure it. Repeat, twisting at least three more handfuls of cloth on the front and

several on the back of the T-shirt. The more twisted sections of cloth you make, the more colorful rings will appear on the final shirt.

4. Have an adult slip on the rubber gloves before placing the shirt in the bleach water. The adult should push the shirt underwater. Soak it for about 5 minutes.

5. Have the adult, still wearing rubber gloves, transfer the shirt from the bleach water to the rinse water. Wait 5 minutes, then squeeze out the excess water.

6. Without removing the rubber bands, hang the shirt up or spread it out on newspapers to dry in the sun.

7. After the shirt has dried for an hour, remove the rubber bands and finish drying.

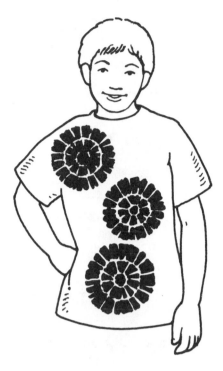

BRAIN BOOSTER

Overall, the shirt became a paler shade of its former color, with darker rings—the centers of the twisted handfuls of cloth. Bleach causes colors to lighten by attacking coloring pigments and breaking them down. If you've ever seen something that's faded after being exposed to the sun, you've discovered the oldest method used to bleach cloth. In the eighteenth century, people began to use chemicals to remove color. Solutions of potash and lye were among the first chemicals used for this job. Today what is called bleach is usually chlorine. This chemical's ability to remove color was first discovered in 1785 by the French chemist Claude Louis Berthollet.

BONUS PACK

Lemon juice is a color remover that you can drink. To see it in action, brew black tea (such as Lipton's orange pekoe and black tea, or any similar tea). Pour this into a white cup, in order to get the best view of the reaction. Then pour in 1 teaspoon of lemon juice. Just like magic, the tea should appear lighter in color. The chemicals, called tannins, that made the tea appear dark were broken down by the lemon juice. Since lemon also adds a nice flavoring to tea, enjoy drinking your "bleached" tea.

Trap Water for Plants ②

Discover a chemical reaction that you can use to water plants while you're not home.

FUEL UP

scissors
3 clean, super-absorbent diapers
mixing bowl
flower pot
potting soil
small plant
*self-sealing plastic sandwich bag (This is used in the Bonus Pack activity.)

BLAST OFF!

1. Using scissors, cut open the diapers.
2. Pour the crystals from 1 diaper into the mixing bowl. These are the "Test Crystals."
3. Fill the flowerpot two-thirds full of soil.
4. Mix the crystals from the remaining 2 diapers into the soil.
5. Dig a hole in the potting soil and move the plant to the pot.
6. Add water until the soil feels moist to the touch. Add water to the Test Crystals until they won't soak up any more, and water puddles around them. Drain off this water.
7. Don't water the plant again for the same number of days that it takes the Test Crystals to dry out and no longer appear swollen.

BRAIN BOOSTER

The crystals are made from a chemical called polyacrylamide. The molecules that make up this chemical are hooked together into long, coiled chains. The natural folds in these chains hold water just as the spaces in a sponge do. Water tends to move from where there is a lot to where there is only a little. As the plant's roots took in water, the soil around the crystals dried out. Then the water that was stored in the molecular chains moved into the soil and was drawn into the plant.

Bonus Pack

Cut open another super-absorbent diaper and pour the crystals into a self-sealing plastic sandwich bag. Examine the size and the feel of the crystals before and after you add 1 teaspoon of water. Add more water, 1 teaspoon at a time, shaking after each addition. Find out how much water the crystals can absorb. Stop when some water remains in the bag. Next, pour the crystals out onto a paper towel. Check each day to see how much time passes before the crystals no longer appear swollen—a sign that they've dried out.

Sun Day Your Prints Will Come ③

Investigate how light can affect chemicals; then get creative with sunlight.

Fuel Up

2 sheets poster board
masking tape
marking pen
sunprint paper (available at craft stores or through the Discovery Corner,
   c/o Lawrence Hall of Science, #5200 University of California, Berkeley,
   CA 94720-5200 (e-mail: lhsstore@uclink4.berkeley.edu)
newspapers
cake pan
water

Blast Off!

1. Fold each sheet of poster board in half and tape three sides shut, forming a big envelope. Mark an "X" on one envelope.

2. In a dimly lit room, transfer the sunprint paper from its package to the poster board envelope with the X on it.

3. Bring the envelope of sunprint paper outdoors, and collect items with interesting shapes that will lie flat, such as leaves, twigs, and flowers.

4. Take out 1 sheet of sunprint paper and quickly arrange the items you collected in a decorative pattern on the paper.

5. Wait for 5 minutes or as long as the sunprint paper instructions state. Then remove the items and slip the paper into the unmarked envelope.

6. Indoors, cover the work area with newspaper and set the cake pan on the papers.

7. Fill the cake pan with water. Rinse each sunprint paper in the water, one at a time, for about 1 minute.

BRAIN BOOSTER

Sunprint paper is really cyanotype paper—paper treated with chemicals that change color when exposed to light. Rinsing the paper in water removes the chemicals from the unexposed areas, the places that were covered by objects placed on the paper. If unwashed, the areas of the paper that were blocked from the light would eventually turn color, too, if the paper were exposed to light. Printing this way is like making shadows in reverse. The paper becomes dark everywhere that it's exposed to sunlight and becomes light where the objects blocked the light.

BONUS PACK

Arrange natural objects, such as leaves, on the sunprint paper in patterns that form letters—for example, one for each letter of a child's name. Mount these on white mat board and make a frame by cutting a rectangular section out of a piece of corrugated cardboard.

Sail a Self-Powered Dragon Boat ③

Build bottle boats powered by a chemical reaction. Then race them in a wading pool.

FUEL UP

scissors
paper towel
1 tablespoon baking soda

empty, clean plastic drink bottle with screw-on cap
hammer and nail or power drill (for adult use only)
flexible plastic straw
modeling clay
colored, permanent marking pens
¼ cup vinegar
wading pool

BLAST OFF!

1. Use scissors to cut the paper towel into fourths.

2. Put the baking soda on one paper towel square. Roll into a packet and twist the ends shut.

3. Have an adult make a hole in the bottle cap, using a hammer and nail or a power drill. The hole should be just big enough for the flexible straw to slide through.

4. Insert the straw. Pack modeling clay around the straw on the inside of the cap to seal any leaks. Plug the straw with a wad of clay.

5. Use the colored marking pens to turn the bottle into a dragon by adding eyes, a tooth-filled mouth, and scales.

6. Pour the vinegar into the bottle and put on the lid.

7. Outdoors, fill the wading pool with water.

8. When you're ready to launch the boat, remove the cap, drop in the packet of baking soda, and screw on the cap.

9. Set the boat on the water, with the straw aimed up and back. Then remove the clay plug.

10. Watch the dragon take off!

BRAIN BOOSTER

There are weak acids in many foods, and vinegar is acetic acid. Baking soda is another kind of chemical called a base. When bases and acids combine, they react. The reaction between baking soda and an acid produces carbon dioxide gas. You can see this reaction by dripping vinegar onto baking soda. The fizzing is caused by the production of carbon dioxide gas. In this activity, the carbon dioxide gas was generated inside the bottle boat and could escape only through the straw. As is stated in one of Newton's laws of motion, for every action there is an equal and opposite reaction. So the force of the gas exiting backward propelled the bottle boat forward.

Bonus Pack

Build a second boat. Divide the family into teams and challenge the teams to figure out ways to make their dragon boat the fastest in the pool. One method might be to add more baking soda and more vinegar to make more gas. Rinse out the bottle boat and power it up again, using 2 tablespoons of baking soda and ½ cup of vinegar.

Whip Up Your Own Chalk ③

Investigate how water can turn a powder into a rock. Then kids can use the rocks they make to create sidewalk masterpieces.

Fuel Up

scissors
toilet paper tube (or small paper cup)
clean, empty half-gallon (2-l) plastic bottle
½ cup plaster of Paris
3 teaspoons acrylic paint (or 1 tablespoon tempera paint powder)
¼ cup cold water
metal spoon
paper towel

Blast Off!

1. Using scissors, cut the toilet paper tube in half to form two short tubes.
2. Cut the top off the plastic bottle.
3. Working outdoors, pour the plaster of Paris, paint, and water into the plastic bottle. Stir with a spoon until well mixed. Add a little water or plaster powder as needed to make the mixture as thick as mashed potatoes.
4. Have a partner hold one of the short tubes vertically, with one end on the ground. Pack the tube with the plaster.
5. Repeat, using different colored paints to make other colors of chalk.
6. Lay the tubes down on their sides and let them dry completely (about 2 hours).

7. Peel the paper tube down to expose the chalk. Use the chalk to create pictures by rubbing it on a cement sidewalk. Peel the paper down farther as needed.

Brain Booster

Plaster of Paris is really a pow-dered rock—gypsum. This type of rock contains water. To make plas-ter of Paris powder, the gypsum is heated to remove the water; then the remaining material is crushed. When water is added to the powder, the molecules of the hard material become bonded together again. That restores the gypsum to its rocklike form. This plaster is called plaster of Paris because the gypsum that was first used to make the powder came from Montmartre in Paris, France.

Bonus Pack

Try adding 1 teaspoon of table salt when you mix up the plaster powder. It makes the plaster harden faster because it helps the water molecules and the plaster molecules bond together. Time how much faster the salted powder hardens. Try adding more or less salt to see how this varies the hardening time.

Grow a Crystal Garden ③

Use a chemical reaction to create something that grows and then changes every time it rains.

Fuel Up

¼ cup table salt
¼ cup water
1 tablespoon household ammonia
¼ cup laundry bluing (available at grocery stores in the laundry soap area)
mixing bowl
metal spoon
disposable aluminum pie pan

rock
scissors
old sponge
red, blue, green, and yellow food coloring

BLAST OFF!

1. Pour the salt, water, ammonia, and bluing into the bowl and mix with a metal spoon.

2. On a sunny day, place the aluminum pie pan outdoors in an open area. Set the rock on the pan to weigh it down.

3. Using scissors, cut the sponge into chunks and fit these around the rock.

4. Spoon the mixture onto the sponge and the rock.

5. Drip on at least 6 drops of each color of food coloring.

6. Check daily.

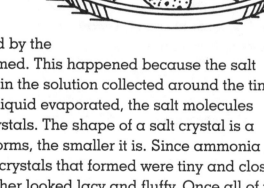

BRAIN BOOSTER

As long as the weather remained dry, **crystals** (solids with a regular shape determined by the arrangement of their atoms) formed. This happened because the salt molecules that were suspended in the solution collected around the tiny particles of bluing. Then as the liquid evaporated, the salt molecules arranged themselves to form crystals. The shape of a salt crystal is a cube, but the faster the crystal forms, the smaller it is. Since ammonia speeds up evaporation, the salt crystals that formed were tiny and close together. All of the crystals together looked lacy and fluffy. Once all of the liquid evaporated, crystal production stopped. However, if it happened to rain during this time, the crystals broke down, the chemicals moved into solution, and crystal production started all over again.

BONUS PACK

Grow a second garden using all of the same ingredients except bluing. Compare the two gardens to see how the crystal development is similar and how it is different.

CHAPTER 6

Physics in the Backyard

Blow Super Soap Bubbles ③

First, blow into water with a straw to discover that bubbles are air trapped inside the skin of something, such as water. A rubber balloon is like a bubble that's limited by the size of its rubber skin. On the other hand, a soap bubble can be as big as you can make the soap bubble film stretch. As a family, why don't you accept the challenge of seeing how big a soap bubble can be?

FUEL UP

pipe cleaner
pliers
coat hanger
scissors
paper cup
piece of paper
tape
a batch of Super Bubble Brew (see the box on page 80)
shallow pan, such as a jellyroll pan or a cake pan

THAT'S AMAZING

According to the Guinness Book of World Records, *Fan Yang of Canada created a bubble wall 156 feet (47.7 m) long and 13 feet (4 m) high in the Kingdome Pavilion in Seattle, Washington, on August 11, 1997. The bubble wall lasted just over 5 seconds before it burst.*

BLAST OFF!

1. Make a number of different bubble-blowing tools by following these directions.

   ● Shape the pipe cleaner into a loop with a handle.

   ● Have an adult use pliers to do the same thing with the coat hanger.

- Using scissors, cut the bottom off the paper cup.
- Roll the paper into a cone, secure the shape with tape, and snip off the point.

2. Working outdoors on a nearly windless day, pour the Super Bubble Brew into the shallow pan.

3. The first time you dip any bubble blower into the solution, hold it there for a count of 10. That will let the rim pick up the solution.

4. Use each bubble maker to see which one can make the biggest soap bubble.

Brain Booster

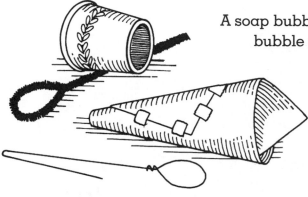

A soap bubble forms when air is forced against the film of bubble solution. When the bubble is filled, it will pull away from the bubble blower. Eventually, part of the bubble's skin will dry, making a hole in the film of solution, and the bubble will burst. Or the bubble will float until it hits an object and pops.

Bonus Pack

Go on a scavenger hunt to collect other things you might use to blow super-big bubbles. You might try these: a toilet paper tube, the plastic rings that hold drink cans together, and a paper plate with the center cut out. Be sure to check with an adult to see if what you've collected is safe for you to test. Then try to blow the biggest bubbles you can.

Super Bubble Brew

Mix together ⅓ cup of water, ⅓ cup of dishwashing liquid (Dawn or Joy work best), and 1 tablespoon of glycerin (available at most grocery stores or pharmacies). The glycerin helps to keep the bubble from drying out quickly, so that the bubble lasts longer. You can substitute corn syrup for glycerin, but glycerin works better.

What Sinks and What Floats? ①

Discover why some things float and some don't.

Fuel Up

    scissors
    clean, empty half gallon (2-l) clear plastic bottle
    water
    permanent marking pen
    2 plastic grocery bags
    test objects: pebble, ice cube, wooden block, Styrofoam cup, ball of modeling clay, coin

Blast Off!

1. Using scissors, cut the top off the plastic bottle.

2. Outdoors, fill the bottle two-thirds full of water.

3. Use the marking pen to draw a line at the water's surface. Also label one grocery bag "Sinks" and the other "Floats."

4. Put one test object in the water. If it sinks, take it out and put it in the "Sinks" bag. If it floats, check how much of the object is below the waterline before you put it in the "Floats" bag.

5. When you have tested all of the items, take another look at the sinkers and think about what they have in common.

6. Take another look at the floaters and decide what they have in common.

Brain Booster

You'll have discovered that many floaters don't just ride on the surface. In fact, an object sinks until it displaces or pushes away enough water to support itself. If an object goes underwater before it can push enough to keep any part of itself above the surface, it sinks.

Bonus Pack

Decide which of the following three balloons will sink: one full of air, one half full of water, or one completely full of water. Test them

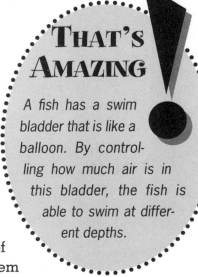

That's Amazing

A fish has a swim bladder that is like a balloon. By controlling how much air is in this bladder, the fish is able to swim at different depths.

in a wading pool or a bathtub to find out if you were right. Air is lighter than water, and you'll discover that the more air an object contains, the higher it floats in the water.

Fly a Paper Bag

Even the youngest explorers can enjoy this activity as they discover what makes kites fly.

FUEL UP

large paper bag (such as a grocery bag)
transparent tape
hole punch
crayons
scissors
20 feet (6 m) of string
toilet paper tube
plastic grocery bags

BLAST OFF!

1. At the open end of the paper grocery bag, put tape strips on the center top of the front and back panels.

2. Also put tape strips on the center top of the two side panels of the bag.

3. Use the hole punch to make a hole in each piece of tape.

4. Use crayons to color the bag and maybe give it a face.

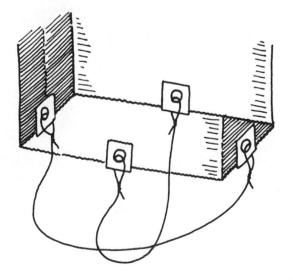

5. With scissors, cut two 30-inch (75-cm) pieces of string.

6. Tie one string so that it connects the two holes in the bag's front panel.

7. Tie the other string so that it connects the two holes in the bag's side panels.

8. Tie one end of the remaining string to the point where the two string loops cross each other.

9. Thread the other end of the string through the toilet paper tube. Tie the free end to the string, forming a loop. Wrap the string around the toilet paper tube.

10. Cut 4 streamers from the plastic bags. Tape two to the front and two to the back panel of the grocery bag.

11. Outdoors on a windy day, try flying the kite. Start by opening the bag so that it will catch the **wind**, the moving air, then place the kite on the ground. Slip a hand through the loop to keep the kite from getting away. While holding onto the handle, slowly walk away from the kite. Once it's airborne, feed the string off the toilet paper tube reel.

Brain Booster

All kites fly because the air flowing over the upper surface is moving faster than the air flowing over the lower surface. Faster-moving air has less **air pressure** (the downward force exerted by the weight of the overlying air) than slower-moving air has, so the air with greater pressure below the kite pushed it upward.

Bonus Pack

Tape the front and back panels of the bag together to create a single paper sheet. Then test how this change affects the kite's flight.

Take the Bounce Out of a Baseball ②

Find out for yourself why professional baseball teams have rules that make sure no one chills the game balls.

Fuel Up

cooler with cold packs (or 4 towels wrapped around a bag of ice)
at least 2 baseballs (5 is best)
measuring stick

Blast Off!

1. Do this outdoors on a warm, sunny day. Conduct the tests on a paved area, like a driveway or a sidewalk.

2. Chill the baseballs by putting them in the cooler for an hour.

3. Have one person hold the measuring stick straight up, with the starting end on the pavement.

4. Have other family members take turns dropping a ball from the top of the stick. Someone will need to watch exactly how high the ball bounces. Each ball should be tested at least two times.

5. Spend 5 minutes doing anything you can think of to safely warm up the baseballs. Possible strategies include holding the ball between two cupped hands, bouncing the ball, and rubbing the ball.

6. Repeat the bounce test with the warmed balls.

7. Compare how high the chilled versus the warmed balls bounced.

Brain Booster

How far a ball bounces depends on two things: the amount of energy transferred to the ball by the impact against the hard surface, and how quickly the elastic material inside the ball snaps back, pushing it away from the hard surface. When a bat strikes a baseball, the ball is compressed to about one half of its original diameter. But the material inside a baseball loses some of its elasticity, or spring, when it's cold.

In 1965, this caused a big scandal when the Detroit Tigers accused the Chicago White Sox of refrigerating the balls given to their pitchers. Then the White Sox accused the Tigers of heating the balls used by their own pitchers. Until that time, in the Major League, the home team supplied the baseballs as they were needed during the game. Today, the home team is required to supply all the baseballs to be used during the game 2 hours before game time. That way, they are all guaranteed to be the same temperature.

Bonus Pack

Give a new twist to playing catch. Start with a plastic jug, such as a half-gallon-sized (2-l) milk container. Cut away the plastic just below the handle to create the scoop. Make one scoop per player. Let your children use markers and strips of colorful tape to decorate each scoop. Then play catch, tossing and catching a tennis ball from scoop to scoop. Let each player score 1 point per catch. Or play a game of "Donkey," where players collect one letter of this animal's name each time they miss a catch. The winner is the player with the fewest letters, once someone has collected all of the letters to spell "D-O-N-K-E-Y."

Find a Bat's Sweet Spot ②

Discover how to find that one special spot, called the sweet spot, on a baseball bat. When that spot makes contact with the ball, the impact causes the least amount of vibrations in the bat. This means that the greatest possible amount of energy is transferred to the ball. It's worth knowing how to locate the sweet spot before you start to play ball.

Fuel Up

at least 2 wooden baseball bats
small hammer

Blast Off!

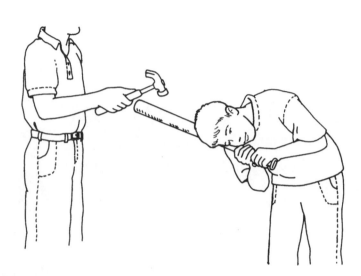

1. Put your hand on the bat near the handle end.

2. Feel for vibrations while an adult taps the bat gently with the hammer. Have the adult start tapping at the bat's fattest end.

3. Call for the tapping to stop when the vibrations or quivering feels the least intense. Mark the spot that was tapped with masking tape.

4. Now put your ear against the bat near the handle end.

5. Listen while an adult partner taps the bat gently with the hammer, starting at the fattest end and moving slowly toward you, the listener.

6. Call for the tapping to stop when the sound seems to change slightly. Mark the spot that was tapped with the masking tape.

Brain Booster

Both marked spots should be in the same or nearly the same place. The sweet spot is about 6 inches (15 cm) away from the fattest part of the bat toward the handle. The term *sweet spot* is used to describe the point on the bat where a moving ball striking the bat sends no stinging sensation to the batter's hands. When struck by a moving ball, the wooden bat vibrates much the same way that a plucked violin string moves. These vibrations rob the bat of some of its energy and thus its striking force. Hitting the ball at the point on the bat that vibrates the least gives the batter's strike maximum impact.

BONUS PACK

Now that you know where the sweet spot is, use that knowledge to play Rounders, a game that's said to have been the inspiration for today's baseball. One thing that's handy about Rounders is that any number of players can be on a team. Just decide whether you want to play with three or five bases. Put old pillows for bases in a circle at any distance apart you choose. From then on, the game is played like baseball, with a pitcher tossing a baseball to a batter and fielders trying to tag runners out. But players each get just one chance to bat, and if they get a strike, they keep on running until they are tagged out. The team that's up to bat also keeps on batting until everyone on the team has had a turn. Then the sides switch. After both teams have had a chance to bat, the winner is the team with the most runners to have made it all the way around the bases.

THAT'S AMAZING

It's not uncommon for the ball to leave a Major Leaguer's bat traveling about 100 miles (160 km) per hour.

Launch Jellybean Missiles ②

Discover how a catapult operates while you take aim at a backyard target.

FUEL UP

2 large spoons (such as mixing spoons)
3 large rubber bands
1 3-by-1-inch (7.5-by-2.5-cm) block of wood
safety goggles
jellybeans

BLAST OFF!

1. Hold the spoons back to back.

2. Slide one rubber band over the two spoons, make a second loop, and slide it about halfway up the handles.

3. Wrap the two other rubber bands around both spoons about 1 inch (2.5 cm) from the end of the handles. Make as many loops as it takes to tightly hold the two spoons together.

4. Have an adult push the two spoon bowls apart just far enough to slide the wood block between the two spoon handles. Push the block through right behind the rubber band wrapped around the middle of the spoon handles.

5. Position the block so that an equal amount sticks out on either side of the handles.

6. Outdoors and away from any people or obstacles, put on safety goggles and, with one hand, hold the catapult by the wood block so that the tips of the handles are aimed away from you.

7. To launch a jellybean, put one in the bowl of the top spoon, pull down on the end of that spoon's bowl, and release it.

8. Watch how far the jellybean travels and brainstorm how to make it go even farther.

9. Check with an adult to be sure your idea is safe, then test it.

Brain Booster

As the spoon sprang back, the jellybean was launched into the air. Then as the jellybean flew through the air, **friction** (the resistance of the air on the jellybean) slowed it down. Soon the jellybean was no longer traveling fast enough to resist **gravity** (the force that pulls everything on Earth toward the ground). Then it dropped. The path the jellybean followed as it soared and then fell is called its **trajectory**. You'll undoubtedly come up with other strategies to make the jellybean fly farther, but one is to use a spoon that bends more easily. A springier spoon will apply more force as it springs back, launching the jellybean farther.

Bonus Pack

Create a target by drawing a chalk circle on a paved area or making a rope circle on the grass. Take turns trying to launch jellybeans to land inside the circle. You can also score points for getting close. To keep track, have one person launch only red jellybeans, another launch only green, and so forth.

Play Water Warriors ③

This is a great game of tag for a hot day. It demonstrates what happens when water is put under pressure.

FUEL UP

hammer and nail or power drill (for adult use only)
clean, empty half-gallon (2-l) plastic bottle with screw-on cap for each player
water
safety pins
paper towels

BLAST OFF!

1. Have an adult use the hammer and nail or a power drill to make a hole in the bottle cap that is the size of a four-penny nail.

2. Fill the bottle with water and screw on the cap.

3. Have each player use 2 safety pins—one on the top and one on the bottom—to attach a paper towel to the front of his or her shirt.

4. Divide the players into two teams.

5. The goal of each team is to eliminate the other team's players by blasting them with water. A player is out when either he or his paper towel gets wet.

6. To fire the water blaster, aim the cap at the target and squeeze the bottle. The harder the squeeze, the farther the stream of water will shoot.

BRAIN BOOSTER

Squeezing shrank the volume of the container (the amount of space that's inside it). Because the space was smaller, the container could no longer hold as much air and water as it did before, so some of the air and the water was pushed out through the hole in the cap. When you stopped squeezing, the container's size increased again, so air rushed into the container through the hole to fill up the space inside. The more pressure, the greater the force pushing the water out the hole, so the water squirted out farther.

BONUS PACK

Line up empty plastic cups on a box and try to hit this target with the water bottle shooter while standing a set distance away. The winner of each round is the person to hit the most cups during his or her turn.

Make a String Phone ③

Long before there were cell phones, kids used string phones to communicate with friends. Build one to find out how it works.

FUEL UP

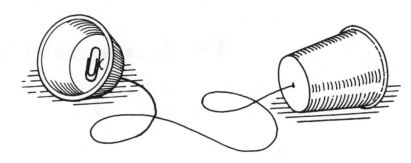

pencil
2 sturdy paper cups
12 feet (3.6 m) of strong string
2 paper clips

BLAST OFF!

1. Use the pencil to mark the center bottom of each cup.

2. Use the pencil's point to poke a small hole where you marked the cup bottom.

3. Thread one end of the string through the hole from the outside to the inside of one cup. Tie that end to a paper clip.

4. Thread the other end of the string through the other cup the same way and tie it to the other paper clip.

5. Outdoors, have two people each take a paper cup and walk away until the string is stretched tight between them. While one person holds the cup to his or her ear, the other person puts the cup over his or her mouth and talks. Switch the position of the cups, so that both people can take turns listening and talking.

BRAIN BOOSTER

Sounds are **vibrations**, movements of molecules that follow the same path over and over. These can travel through solids, liquids, or water, but they travel best through solids. In this experiment, when someone spoke into a phone cup, his or her voice pushed out waves of air that made the bottom of the cup vibrate. These vibrations traveled along the string to the other cup and made the bottom of listener's cup vibrate. That created waves of air that reached the listener's ear. The listener's ear detected these and sent messages to the brain. In a flash, the brain interpreted these messages as sounds. *Note: The string has to be really tight for the vibrations to stay strong enough to move the bottom of the listener's cup.*

BONUS PACK

Brainstorm ways to modify your paper cup phone system that might improve how well you can hear. You'll think of more ways, but here are some to consider: use monofilament fishing line instead of string, use plastic cups, or use tin cans.

Peek around Corners ②

Make a tool to look over bushes and around corners, while you discover how light is reflected.

FUEL UP

kitchen knife (for adult use only)
2 half-gallon (2-l) cartons
protractor
ruler
marking pen
2 small, flat mirrors about as wide as the carton
scissors
duct tape

BLAST OFF!

1. Have an adult use the knife to cut the top off each milk carton.

2. On the front panel (label side) of one carton, have the adult cut out a 2-inch (5-cm) square near the bottom of the carton.

3. Place this carton on its side so that the cut-out square faces your right hand.

4. Place the protractor with its straight edge along the bottom of what is now the top panel. Make a mark at a 45-degree angle along the left-hand edge of this panel.

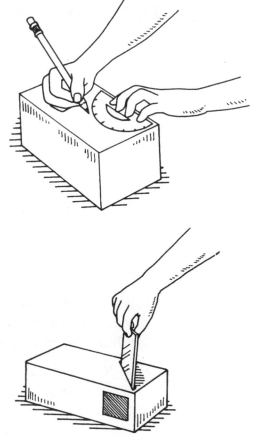

5. Using a ruler, draw a straight line from the bottom right corner toward this mark. Make the line whatever length is needed to let one of the mirrors slide into the carton. Use scissors to cut along this line. Enlarge the line to a slot the width of the mirror.

6. Slide the mirror into the slot, with the reflective surface aimed at the carton's top. When you hold this carton up and look into the cut-out square, you should now see whatever is straight above you. Tape the side of the carton to anchor the mirror in place.

7. Repeat steps 2 through 6 with the second milk carton and the other mirror.

8. Place the second carton on top of the first one. Turn the cartons so that the cut-out square in the upper one is on the opposite side of the one on the bottom.

9. Use duct tape to anchor the two cartons together where they meet, forming a tower. This is now a periscope.

10. Use the periscope to see what's on the other side of an obstacle or around the corner of a building.

Brain Booster

Light travels in a straight line and is reflected or bounced off a shiny object, such as a mirror. A periscope works by reflecting light between two mirrors and then to the viewer's eyes. The key thing is to have the mirrors positioned at just the right angle to reflect light from one mirror to the other. A 45-degree angle seems to be the right angle to make this happen.

Bonus Pack

Use a mirror to send coded messages as flashes of reflected sunlight. When a mirror is used this way, it's called a heliograph. In the 1870s, General Nelson A. Miles established heliograph stations on mountain peaks in New Mexico and Arizona, creating a network to keep track of warring Apache Indians. Of course, you'll have to make up your own family code for flashing messages. For example, two long flashes followed by one short could mean "Time to come home for dinner."

For More Science in the Backyard Fun

Baby Einstein: Nature Discovery Cards by Julie Aigner-Clark (Glendale, Calif.: Baby Einstein Company, 2003). Discovery cards present 29 learning experiences that introduce nature basics. Ages 4 and up.

DK Nature Encyclopedia by Dorling Kindersley Publishing (New York: DK Publishing, 1998). Amazing facts and lots of illustrations introduce weird animals and little known facts about familiar animals. Ages 9–12.

Fun with Nature: Take-Along Guide by Mel Boring (Clanhassen, Minn.: North Word Press, 1999). Illustrations accompany easy-to-follow information sections about animals and plants. Ages 9–12.

How Nature Works/100 Ways Parents and Kids Can Share the Secrets of Nature by David Burnie (Chappaqua, N.Y.: Reader's Digest, 1991). Hands-on activities are fun for children and adults to share. Full-color photos add to the experiences. Ages 8–12.

The Gardening Book by Jane Bull (New York: DK Publishing, 2003). Kids discover what plants need to grow, plus they get tips on choosing plants. Ages 5–10.

The Kids' Nature Book: 365 Indoor/Outdoor Activities and Experiences (Williamson Kids Can! Series) by Susan Milord (Charlotte, Vt.: Williamson Publishing, 1996). A project a day keeps kids investigating and discovering. Ages 7 and up.

The Kids' Book of Weather Forecasting: Build a Weather Station, Read the Sky, and Make Predictions! by Mark Breen and Kathleen Friestad (Charlotte, Vt.: Williamson Publishing, 2000). Experiments and directions for making weather instruments from easy-to-find materials. Ages 9–12.

Why? The Best Ever Question and Answer Book about Nature, Science and the World around You by Catherine Ripley (Toronto, Ontario: Owl Communications, 2001). This book is packed with information about lots of things that kids and adults might wonder about. Ages 4–10.

PART III
Science in a Minute

Trick your brain into seeing a hole in your hand and a piece of finger floating in front of your nose. Turn milk into a swirling rainbow. Make a glass produce a bell-like tone when you rub it. Stick a pin into a balloon without popping it. And lots more! These activities don't take long to set up and do, but they're full of discovery fun.

CHAPTER 7

Biology in a Minute

Look through a Hole in Your Hand ②

Investigate what happens when your two eyes look at very different views.

FUEL UP

sheet of paper or anything that can be rolled into a tube—or use a toilet paper tube

BLAST OFF!

1. Roll the paper into a long tube.

2. Hold the tube in your right hand and look straight through it with your right eye.

3. Hold your left hand up—palm toward your face—about 6 inches (15 cm) from your face.

4. Look straight at your left palm with your left eye.

5. Keep looking straight through the tube and at your palm. What do you see?

6. Switch, holding the tube in the left hand and looking at your right palm. Decide whether the effect is the same as before or if it's different.

BRAIN BOOSTER

The effect was like looking at the world through a hole in your left hand. You saw an object when light reflecting off the object reached light-sensitive cells in the back of your eye.

These cells send messages to your brain. Then your brain analyzes the messages. Usually, your brain receives nearly identical messages from each eye. This time, though, the right and left eyes sent very different messages. Analyzing these, the brain blended the messages so that it looked like you had a hole in your hand.

BONUS PACK

Try looking through a short tube and then a long tube. Decide whether using a longer tube keeps this illusion from happening.

See a Ghostly Floating Finger ③

Try this to trick your eyes. It's especially eerie because the ghostly floating finger is your own.

BLAST OFF!

1. Hold up both hands so that your two index fingers are touching.

2. Touch the joined index fingers to your nose.

3. Look at something in the distance over the top of the joined index fingers.

4. Keep looking at the same thing while slowly moving the joined index fingers away from your nose.

5. When the joined fingers reach about 6 to 8 inches (15 to 20 cm) away from your nose, you'll see something freaky.

BRAIN BOOSTER

You saw what looked like a piece of one finger floating between the two fingertips. The floating piece of finger was an illusion, something that seemed to be there but wasn't. It happened because of the way human eyes focus. When light enters your eye, it passes through a lens. Muscles change the shape of the lens as your eye shifts its focus from close to far-away objects. The light is focused on light-sensitive cells at the back of the eye. These send messages to your brain, and when your brain analyzes these messages, you become aware of the image. Of course, that happens almost instantly, and the eye muscles adjust the shape of the lens quickly, too. Usually, your brain receives only one set of messages at a time—images for a close-up image or those for an image that is far away. This time, though, the brain received both close up and far away image messages at the same time. Processing these two at once created the illusion of the floating finger.

BONUS PACK

How close can an object get before you can no longer focus on it? Find out. Hold up a finger and focus on it. Slowly bring that finger toward the center of your face. How close can you bring your finger before it starts to look blurry? Have someone use a measuring tape to find out the exact distance. This distance is determined by how well the lens's shape can be adjusted. Have different family members try the test. Compare the results between younger and older family members.

Find Your Center of Gravity ③

Discover what's called the **center of gravity**, the point around which a body's or an object's weight is evenly distributed in all directions, and how this affects you.

FUEL UP

apple

BLAST OFF!

1. Stand against a wall with the backs of your heels and your rear touching the wall.

2. Have someone place the apple on the floor about 1 foot (0.3 m) away from your feet.

3. Bend over to pick up the apple, but do it without moving your feet and rear end or bending your knees.

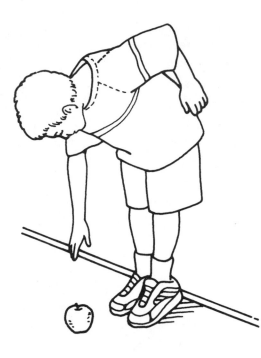

4. As soon as you feel like you're going to fall over, move your feet until you feel balanced again.

5. Look back to see how far away from the wall you moved in order to keep your balance.

BRAIN BOOSTER

Center of gravity is the point around which an object's weight is evenly distributed in all directions. For the human body, it's over the body's support base. For a gymnast, that could be whatever body parts are being used for support. When you stood up, your center of gravity was straight above your body's feet. Bending over without bending your knees or repositioning your body shifted a lot of weight in front of the body's center of gravity. Moving your feet forward replaced this support base directly under the main part of your body's weight in its new position.

BONUS PACK

Fold a 3-by-5-inch (7.5-by-12.5-cm) index card in half lengthwise and cut out an oval at this center point.

Use transparent tape to attach one small coin, like a penny, on either side of this cutout. Place the cut-out area of the card on your outstretched index finger. With the weight distributed on either side of your finger, the card should stay balanced. Try walking and observe any shifts you need to make to keep the card's center of gravity directly over your finger. Just for fun, draw and color a face on the balancing card.

Feel the Sound ③

Discover that sound can be felt as well as heard.

FUEL UP

2 16-inch (40-cm) pieces of sturdy string
metal coat hanger

BLAST OFF!

1. Tie one end of each string to the bottom of the coat hanger.

2. Slide one string to the left until it meets the side of the hanger.

3. Slide the other string just as far to the right.

4. Wrap one string around each of your index fingers.

5. Put these fingertips into your ears.

6. Let the dangling hanger bump gently into each of these items one at a time: the edge of a wooden table, the side of a metal saucepan, a big soft pillow, and a glass windowpane.

7. Think about how each sound feels and how it sounds.

BRAIN BOOSTER

Sounds start when something vibrates or moves back and forth. The vibrations travel through solids, liquids, and gases. When those vibrations reach the human ear, they make the ear drum vibrate. This vibration is passed on through a series of tiny bones to special sensors that send signals to the brain. When the brain analyzes these signals, the vibrations are interpreted as sounds. Different objects vibrate differently, so they make different sounds.

BONUS PACK

While a partner keeps his or her eyes closed, make soft sounds on one side of that person. Challenge the listener to point to the sound. Human ears are on opposite sides of the head. This lets sound waves entering one ear reach the brain slightly ahead of sound waves entering the other ear. The brain analyzes the time difference—even fractions of a second—between when it receives messages from each ear. Then it uses the time difference to interpret where the sound came from.

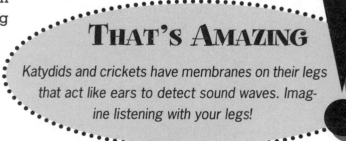

THAT'S AMAZING

Katydids and crickets have membranes on their legs that act like ears to detect sound waves. Imagine listening with your legs!

Identify Mystery Items by Touch Alone ③

This activity will test your touch memory. It will also demonstrate that the sense of touch is more than a measure of pressure.

FUEL UP

blindfold
damp sponge
metal spoon
unsharpened wooden pencil
paperback book
stuffed animal
banana

BLAST OFF!

1. Have a partner gently tie a blindfold over your eyes. Or keep your eyes closed throughout the test.

2. Have the partner hand you the test items one at a time.

3. Using only your fingers, examine each item. As you do, describe how it feels.

4. Based on what you felt, tell what item you think you're holding.

5. Continue until you have felt each item.

BRAIN BOOSTER

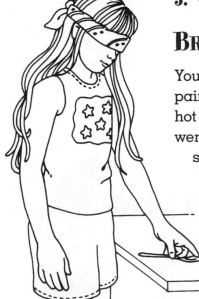

Your skin contains pressure sensors, as well as sensors for heat and pain. It's possible to know if something is slimy, slick, bumpy, soft, furry, hot or cold, and more. You used these clues to guess what object you were holding. Unlike your senses of sight, hearing, taste, and smell, sensors are located everywhere you have skin. So your brain receives information about everything your body touches. To stay safe, the human body has more pain sensors than ones for pressure or temperature.

BONUS PACK

Make a family mystery sock. Push something into the toe of a big cotton tube sock. Be sure it's something that won't cut or scratch. Then challenge the other family members to identify the mystery item by reaching their hands into the sock to feel what's inside. Each week let a different family member take a turn picking a mystery item to challenge the others. Before revealing the item, allow time for all participants to share what features they felt and guess what they think the item is.

Find Out That Some Body Parts Have More Touch Sensors ②

Explain that there are more touch sensors on some parts of the body than on others. Do this test to find out which body parts have more.

FUEL UP

    paper clip
    blindfold
    ruler

BLAST OFF!

1. Bend the paper clip so that the two ends are only about ½ inch (1cm) apart.

2. Have a partner put the blindfold on you or keep your eyes closed throughout the test.

3. Have your partner gently touch both ends of the paper clip to your left thumb at the same time. Say whether you feel one or two points.

4. Repeat, testing each of the following body parts: cheek, inside wrist, ankle, knee, sole of one foot, tip of nose.

BRAIN BOOSTER

It was easier to feel both of the paper clip's points when they were pressed against certain body parts. Some areas of the skin have more sensors than others. The areas with the most touch sensors are the hands, the lips, the face, the neck, the tongue, the fingertips, and the feet. The buttocks and the small of the back have a lot fewer sensors.

THAT'S AMAZING

After awhile, people stop noticing the clothes and the jewelry they wear (unless they're too tight!). When the skin is pressed in the same place for a long time, it stops being as sensitive to that pressure. The brain also starts to ignore these repeated pressure messages.

That makes it possible for us to sit for a long period without the pressure becoming painful.

BONUS PACK

Go on a scavenger hunt around the house to find things that feel rough, smooth, slippery, bumpy, furry, cold, hard, and soft that you can use to make a texture picture—one whose parts are made out of pieces of different materials.

Discover the Value of a Thumb ③

Kids discover just how useful it is to have a thumb, as they enjoy building with egg carton blocks. To get ready for the action, save up egg cartons and collect more from friends.

FUEL UP

tape
at least 2 dozen empty egg cartons
gloves (one pair per person)

BLAST OFF!

1. Tape all of the egg cartons shut.

2. Put on the gloves, but hold your thumbs folded inside and across your palms.

3. Use your gloved hands with no thumbs to stack the cartons into a tower.

4. Repeat, wearing the gloves but this time with the thumbs and the fingers in the correct places.

5. Divide into teams and have a building race without thumbs. Then again with thumbs.

BRAIN BOOSTER

It was a lot harder to stack cartons when you didn't have the use of your thumbs. The human hand consists of the wrist, the palm, four fingers, and a thumb. Humans can grip things, thanks to having a thumb. It's called an "opposable thumb" because it can be moved in the opposite direction of the fingers, making it possible to bring the thumb and the fingers together. The underside of the fingers, the thumb, and the palm are ridged. That helps them to hold on while they grip.

BONUS PACK

To see the value of having a thumb, try these activities without using either thumb:

- Pick up a coin.
- Tear off a piece of tape.
- Tie a shoe.
- Zip up a jacket.
- Turn a faucet on and off.
- Cut meat with a knife and a fork.
- Button a shirt.
- Close a self-sealing plastic bag.
- If you have any chopsticks available, try eating with them.

Trick the Body's
Temperature Sensors ②

Investigate how the body judges whether something is hot or cold.

FUEL UP

3 identical bowls (soup bowls are big enough, but any size will do)
water
ice cubes
table

BLAST OFF!

1. Fill one bowl nearly to the top with very warm tap water.

2. Fill another bowl with cold tap water and add some ice cubes.

3. Fill the third bowl with lukewarm tap water.

4. Line up the three bowls close to one side of the table.

5. Stand in front of the bowls. Place one hand in the hot water and one in the cold water.

6. Have a partner report when 30 seconds has passed.

7. Quickly plunge both hands into the lukewarm water.

8. Think about how the water feels to each hand.

BRAIN BOOSTER

It felt cool to the hand that had been in the hot water. It felt warm to the hand that had been in the cold water. Your skin has sensors that detect heat and cold and send messages to your brain. When your brain analyzes these messages, you become aware of the temperature, but your brain judges hot and cold based only on the difference between the temperature your body has gotten used to and the new temperature being detected by the sensors.

BONUS PACK

Investigate how sweating can cool off your body. Stand at the sink and slip each hand into a cotton sock. Hold just one hand under the faucet until the sock is soaked. Then pull your hand out of the water, but leave it dripping into the sink. Think about which hand feels cooler. It will be the wet hand. As the water evaporates, some of the body's heat energy is used up to change the liquid into a gas. And that has a cooling effect. When your body overheats, it produces sweat, a liquid that comes out onto the surface of your skin. When the sweat evaporates, it takes some of the heat from your body so you feel cooler. What happens when you stand in front of a fan when you're wet? You feel even cooler because the fan causes the liquid to evaporate faster.

Chemistry in a Minute

Make Dark Pennies Gleam ②

Use a quick chemical reaction to clean up your pennies.

FUEL UP

five dark brown pennies
dinner plate or a sturdy paper plate
2 tablespoons salt
¼ cup vinegar

BLAST OFF!

1. Place the pennies on the plate. Put them close together but not overlapping

2. Sprinkle the salt over the pennies.

3. Pour on the vinegar and see what happens.

BRAIN BOOSTER

The dark pennies became bright copper. When copper is in contact with the air, it changes to copper oxide, a chemical that appears dark. Salt contains the chemical chloride. When the chloride combined with a weak acid, like vinegar, the reaction dissolved the dark copper oxide, exposing fresh, shiny copper.

BONUS PACK

Rinse off the shiny copper pennies and place them on a dry paper towel. Check back every few hours to see how long it takes the pennies to turn dark again. It won't be longer than overnight. Brainstorm to think of what you might do to make pennies keep their gleam. Check with an adult to be sure what you want to try is safe. Then try it.

Change Milk into a Swirling Rainbow ③

Start by comparing whole milk, 2% milk, and skim milk. Taste each one and note that the difference in taste comes from the amount of fat in each type of milk. Once the family discovers that milk contains tiny suspended droplets of fat—some more than others—try this activity using whole milk.

FUEL UP

> pie pan
> milk
> red, yellow, blue, and green food coloring
> liquid dishwashing soap

BLAST OFF!

1. Fill the pie pan nearly full of milk.
2. Drip in a few drops of each color of the food coloring.
3. Make a spiral of liquid soap in the center of the pie pan.
4. Watch what happens to the milk.

BRAIN BOOSTER

The colors in the milk started to swirl, moving and mixing. Like water, the surface of the milk had **surface tension**. This means that the molecules at the top tended to cling to each other, forming a sort of "skin." The dishwashing soap broke the bonds between the milk molecules at the surface. The soap then interacted with both the water molecules in milk and the fat molecules suspended in that milk. One end of each soap molecule attached to a fat molecule, and the other end attached to a water molecule. This reaction created currents that made the milk swirl, and that motion mixed the floating drops of food coloring.

Bonus Pack

Repeat this activity using skim milk (which has a low butterfat content) and again with cream, which has a high butterfat content. How does the percentage of fat affect how long this reaction continues?

Whip Up Matter That Is Both a Liquid and a Solid ③

Discover the properties that make matter either a solid or a liquid, while you investigate a mysterious mixture that's a little like both. *Note: When you're finished, throw this matter away in the trash. Do not put it down the drain, as it might clog the pipe.*

Fuel Up

    1 cup cornstarch
    mixing bowl
    food coloring (any color is fine)
    ½ cup water
    mixing spoon
    waxed paper

Blast Off!

1. Pour the cornstarch into the bowl.
2. Drip in about 6 drops of food coloring.
3. Add ¼ cup of water and stir to mix well.
4. Add more water or cornstarch as needed to make a mixture that is firm when poked with a finger but that flows if the bowl is tipped.

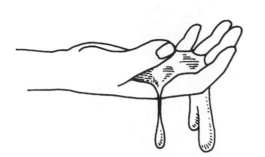

5. Test the mixture's properties to judge whether it behaves like a solid or a liquid. Working over waxed paper, shape some into a ball. Hold the ball to see if it will keep its shape. Hold some in your hand and let it drip through your fingers. Try breaking the mixture. Press the mixture onto the waxed paper and poke it.

BRAIN BOOSTER

These are the properties of liquids and solids that this mixture shares:

Liquids have a definite size but lack a definite shape. They can change shape easily.

Solids have a definite shape and a definite size. They can break but do not change shape easily.

The way this mystery matter formed is that the tiny particles of cornstarch became suspended in the water and stayed suspended. This is a lot like quicksand. Quicksand is sand or soil that's completely saturated with water. In other words, there is so much water that the solid bits are completely surrounded by the water.

BONUS PACK

Examine a liquid and a solid. Then come up with at least three other tests to see if the mystery matter is more like a liquid or a solid.

Save Your Breath—Make a Chemical Fire Extinguisher ②

Start by explaining that a candle needs oxygen, a gas in the air, to burn. Then prove it by producing another gas to block oxygen from reaching a candle flame.

FUEL UP

modeling clay
scissors
clean, empty 1-liter plastic soft drink bottle

birthday cake candle (you can use a candle stub, but be sure it's short enough to be below the rim of the cut-off soda bottle)

matches (for adult use only)

Alka-Seltzer tablet (or other bicarbonate of soda tablet)

¼ cup water

BLAST OFF!

1. Roll the modeling clay in your hands to warm it.

2. Shape the clay into a ball about the size of a small lemon.

3. Using scissors, cut the top off the soda bottle.

4. Press the clay ball into the center of the bottle's bottom.

5. Stick the candle—wick end up—into the clay.

6. Have an adult light the candle.

7. Break the Alka-Seltzer tablet into pieces and place them around the clay at the base of the candle.

8. Pour a ¼ cup of water over the broken tablet, being careful to stay away from the flame.

9. Watch the candle flame as the tablet dissolves and the water bubbles.

BRAIN BOOSTER

The candle went out. When the Alka-Seltzer tablet dissolved, its ingredients began to react with each other. If you read the list of ingredients on the package, you'll find that the Alka-Seltzer tablet contains citric acid and sodium bicarbonate, also called baking soda. Acids react with baking soda to produce carbon dioxide gas. That's what made the water fizz. Carbon dioxide gas is also heavier than air, so it lingers close to where it's produced around the candle. That prevents the oxygen in the air from reaching the candle flame, so the candle eventually goes out. Commercially available household fire extinguishers may contain different chemicals, but those most commonly sold for use in the kitchen contain a powder, such as potassium bicarbonate, and liquid water. Then the extinguisher is pressurized with either nitrogen or carbon dioxide gas. When activated, this gas causes the water and the powder to shoot out in a forceful stream.

BONUS PACK

Repeat the activity, but this time substitute dry ice for the broken Alka-Seltzer tablet. *Caution: Dry ice should be used only with adult supervision. Never touch dry ice with your bare hands.* Dry ice is available where party supplies are sold. Have an adult wear oven mitts and use a spoon to transfer bits of dry ice to the soda bottle. Then pour on water as before and watch what happens. The candle flame goes out because dry ice is frozen carbon dioxide. The water speeds up the melting process, releasing carbon dioxide gas. Then this gas blocks oxygen from reaching the candle, and the flame stops burning.

Stop Apple Slices from Turning Brown ②

Peeled and sliced apples quickly turn brown and lose some of their flavor. Discover a way to keep this from happening.

FUEL UP

    1 apple
    knife (for adult use only)
    bowl
    ¼ cup of lemon juice or orange juice
    paper towel

BLAST OFF!

1. Have an adult peel, core, and slice the apple with a knife.

2. Immediately place all but one of the apple slices in the bowl.

3. Pour on the fruit juice. Turn the slices as needed to make sure all are coated with the juice.

4. Place the apple slice that didn't go into the bowl on the paper towel. That's your control, or the part of an experiment that isn't changed by any kind of a test.

5. Let the slices sit uncovered for an hour.

6. Check the coloring of the slices that were coated with the juice and the one that wasn't coated.

Brain Booster

At least part of the uncoated slice was brown. The slices coated with fruit juice were still light in color. And if you scraped away a little of the brown part of the uncoated slice, you saw that it was still light underneath. Apples, like all living things, are made up of building blocks called **cells**. Peeling and slicing an apple opens up some of its cells. This releases special chemicals called enzymes, which react with oxygen to start breaking down the cells. The result is that the fruit turns brown, and its taste changes. Acids can stop this reaction, and citrus juice contains a mild acid called citric acid.

Bonus Pack

You can also put apple slices in plain water or in saltwater or cover them up in clear plastic wrap. The goal is to prevent oxygen in the air from interacting with the chemical in the fruit's exposed cells. Do any of these methods work as well as the juice does? Why might one of these ideas be a better way to stop apple slices from turning brown?

CHAPTER 9

Physics in a Minute

Make a Penny Move without Touching It ②

Explore how energy can be transferred, while you perform what looks like magic.

FUEL UP

six identical coins
smooth, flat tabletop (one that won't scratch)

BLAST OFF!

1. Line the coins up in a straight row on the tabletop.

2. Move the coins until they are just touching.

3. Slide one coin about 2 inches (5 cm) away from one end of the line.

4. Snap your index finger into the coin hard enough to push it back into the line of coins. If the coin misses the line of coins, try again.

5. What happens when the coin strikes the row of coins?

6. Repeat to see that the same thing happens every time.

BRAIN BOOSTER

When the coin you snapped hit the row of coins, it joined the line again and one coin slid away from the other end of the line. Pushing the coin gave it

momentum or stored-up energy. When the coin hit the first coin in the line, it passed on the energy that hadn't been used up in crossing the table. This energy quickly moved through each coin. At the end of the line, there was still enough left-over energy to move one penny.

BONUS PACK

Repeat this activity, but this time line up two coins and send them sliding into the line of coins. This requires careful aim, so you may need to practice before you succeed. It's worth the effort, though, to see what happens.

Make One Balloon Blow Up Another ②

Perform what looks like magic, as you discover that stretching rubber makes it thinner.

FUEL UP

¼-inch (0.6-cm) drill bit or sharp scissors (for adult use only)
empty plastic film can without its lid
2 identical large rubber balloons
2 pipe cleaners (or long twist ties)

BLAST OFF!

1. Have an adult, using scissors or a drill, cut the bottom off the film can.

2. Blow up one balloon until it is only slightly inflated or about double its original size. Twist the neck to seal.

3. Keep the balloon sealed while an adult rolls the mouth of the balloon over one end of the film can. Twist a pipe cleaner or a twist tie around the neck to keep the balloon sealed.

4. Blow up the other balloon until it's almost fully inflated and keep the balloon sealed while an adult rolls the mouth of the balloon over the other end of the film can. Twist a pipe cleaner or a twist tie around the neck to keep the balloon sealed.

5. Hold the film can between the balloons. Predict which way you think the air will flow between the two balloons.

6. Carefully remove the ties from the two balloons and watch what happens.

BRAIN BOOSTER

You might think that air should have rushed from the nearly full balloon into the nearly empty one. But that isn't what happened. The slightly filled balloon shrank as the air inside it flowed into the almost fully inflated balloon. That happened because the rubber of the less inflated balloon was thicker, providing extra push. That's why it's necessary to blow hard when you start blowing up a balloon. After that, easy puffs are enough to finish. The fuller the balloon becomes, the thinner the stretched rubber is, and the thinner it gets, the less force the rubber exerts on the air inside the balloon.

BONUS PACK

Examine the fully inflated balloon to find one spot where the balloon's skin isn't stretched as thin. It's directly opposite the balloon's mouth. You'll use that in the next activity.

Stick a Pin in a Balloon without Popping It ②

Discover that even solids are made up of individual molecules.

FUEL UP

    3 round rubber balloons
    straight pin
    1 tablespoon vegetable oil in a cup or a bowl
    2 pairs safety goggles

BLAST OFF!

1. Blow into a balloon to inflate it nearly full. Twist and tie the neck to seal.

2. Examine the balloon to find the darkest spot. It will be directly opposite the balloon's mouth.

3. Dip the pin into the vegetable oil.

4. Put on safety goggles. Have an adult put on safety goggles, too.

5. Hold the balloon while the adult pushes the oiled pin into the dark spot on the balloon. This should be done slowly, twisting the pin as it's inserted.

6. If the balloon pops, coat the pin with more oil and try again with another balloon.

BRAIN BOOSTER

Everything is made up of molecules. A balloon's rubbery skin is made up of long chains of molecules. The darker spots on the balloon are places where the molecules are less stretched, so the pin was able to slip between the molecules without tearing the rubbery material. The oil helped it to slip in more easily. Then the stretchy molecules clung to the pin so that piercing the skin didn't cause an air leak.

BONUS PACK

Prove that a balloon's rubber skin is made up of molecules with natural spaces between them. To do this, measure the distance around a newly inflated rubber balloon. Then wait a day and measure again. Surprise! The balloon shrank. That's because air leaked out between the molecules.

Use Your Fingertip to Make a Glass Ring ②

Discover that the ridges that form a fingerprint are enough to start glass vibrating and create sound waves.

FUEL UP

good crystal goblet (check with an adult before using)
water
your finger

Blast Off!

1. Fill the goblet two-thirds full of water.
2. Wet the tip of one index finger by dipping it into the water.
3. Hold the stem of the goblet with your dry hand.
4. Rub the wet fingertip around the goblet's rim. Keep circling the rim rapidly until you hear a sound.

Brain Booster

You heard a bell-like tone. The skin on each fingertip forms a pattern of ridges. These help a person to grip and hold onto things. The ridges were even able to grip the rim of the glass. That grip made it feel as if the fingertip was sticking and then slipping. This motion jerked the glass just enough to make the glass vibrate, which made the air above the water in the glass vibrate. These vibrations created waves of air that were detected by the ears. Then the ears sent messages to the brain, where they were analyzed. The brain interpreted the airwaves as sounds. It's important to use good crystal because you can count on the glass rim to be smooth. The rim of a cheap glass is likely to be slightly irregular. That can disrupt the jerking motion enough to keep vibrations from creating sounds.

Bonus Pack

Repeat, rubbing the rims of goblets that are filled with different amounts of water and listen to how this changes the tone.

Use Air Pressure to Keep Water from Leaking ③

Not only is everything and everyone surrounded by air, this gas constantly exerts pressure in every direction. Try this activity to see air pressure in action.

Fuel Up

clean, empty 2-liter plastic soft drink bottle with screw-on cap
kitchen sink
water
push pin (pin with a large head that's used to tack things on bulletin boards)

BLAST OFF!

1. Set the bottle in the sink.

2. Fill the bottle with water and screw on the cap.

3. Press the pushpin into the side of the bottle. Repeat to make five more holes in the sides of the bottle.

4. Squeeze the bottle. What happens?

5. What happens when you stop squeezing?

6. Repeat, to see what happens each time.

BRAIN BOOSTER

When you squeezed the bottle, water squirted out of the holes, and when you stopped squeezing, the leaks stopped. What seemed like magic was air pressure at work. Even though air is invisible, it takes up space and exerts force in all directions. The force of the air pushing in on the sides of the bottle was enough to keep the water from flowing out the holes. The bottle leaked only when you squeezed to increase the pressure on the water, forcing it out of the holes.

BONUS PACK

Try taking the cap off the bottle. Because air exerts force in all directions, it's now also pushing down on the water inside the bottle. Just as squeezing the bottle created pressure, this creates enough force to push the water out of the holes.

Decrease Air Pressure by Blowing ③

Discover that fast-moving air has less air pressure, and surprise everyone with this activity.

FUEL UP

2 identical round balloons
2 20-inch (50-cm) pieces of string
masking tape

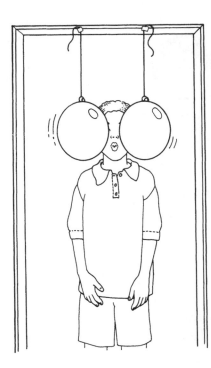

BLAST OFF!

1. Blow up one balloon and tie the neck.

2. Blow up the second balloon to be about as big as the first balloon and tie the neck.

3. Tie a string to the neck of each balloon.

4. Have an adult tape the free ends of the strings to the top of a doorway, so that the balloons hang down side by side, almost—but not quite—touching.

5. Stand directly in front of the pair of balloons.

6. Blow hard between the balloons. What happens?

BRAIN BOOSTER

The balloons moved together. Fast-moving air has less pressure than slower-moving air. Your puff of air decreased the air pressure between the two balloons, so the air with greater pressure surrounding the balloons pushed them together.

BONUS PACK

Brainstorm a way to use air pressure to make the balloons move apart. Check with an adult to be sure your idea is safe and then try it. Remember, if you want to make the balloons move apart, the air pressure between them will need to be greater than the surrounding air pressure.

Blow Out a Candle through a Bottle ②

Discover how a stream of air reacts when it strikes a curved surface.

FUEL UP

table
electrical outlet
2-liter plastic soda bottle
candle in a candle holder (Be sure the candle in the holder is shorter than the bottle.)
matches (for adult use only)
blow dryer

Blast Off!

1. Set the table close to an electrical outlet. Be sure the table is away from any air drafts, which could spoil the results.

2. Set the bottle just a few inches (centimeters) from the edge of the table.

3. Set the candle on the table about 4 inches (10 cm) from the bottle.

4. Have an adult light the candle.

5. Have an adult plug in the blow dryer. Sit or kneel next to the table, directly in front of the bottle. Hold the nozzle of the blow dryer about 5 inches (12.5 cm) from the bottle.

6. While an adult watches the candle, switch on the blow dryer.

7. If this doesn't blow the candle out, switch off the blow dryer. Have the adult help position the blow dryer so that it's aimed at the bottle at the same level as the candle's flame. Then switch on the blow dryer again.

Brain Booster

The stream of air from the blow dryer split when it struck the curved surface. Then the air stream flowed around the curve and reunited into a single stream. This stream of air continued on a straight path and blew out the candle.

Bonus Pack

Try to blow out the candle with your breath by puffing at the bottle. If you are able to make the flame only flutter, have an adult try blowing at the bottle.

Lift Cereal with a Balloon ③

Investigate static electricity to see how it's produced and what it can do.

Fuel Up

2 tablespoons puffed rice cereal
table with a smooth, flat top
round rubber balloon
woolen cloth

BLAST OFF!

1. Pour the cereal onto the table.

2. Blow up the balloon and tie the neck to seal.

3. Rub the inflated balloon back and forth on the wool.

4. Bring the part of the balloon that was rubbed close to the cereal. Watch what happens.

BRAIN BOOSTER

First, you need to know something about electricity. Electricity is caused by charged particles called electrons. Electrons are normally parts of atoms—the building blocks that make up molecules. A molecule is the smallest amount of something that can exist and still have all of its characteristics. Sometimes, electrons are knocked out of their atoms. Then those loose electrons may bump into other atoms and may free still more electrons.

Free electrons may collect in one place or may move from one place to another. When the electrons are in just one place, the charged bits form static electricity. Rubbing the balloon and the wool together knocked free some of the wool atoms' electrons. Then those loose electrons collected as static electricity on the surface of the balloon.

When the charged surface of the balloon approached the table, it attracted the bits of cereal. Then, because the cereal bits were so light, they stuck to the balloon even when it was lifted off the table.

BONUS PACK

Recharge the balloon to see what else it can pick up. Try bits of paper, aluminum foil, and uncooked grains of rice. Try other items. What's the heaviest item that the charged balloon can lift?

Magnify with Water Drops ③

Discover that water drops are **magnifiers**, something that causes objects to appear larger than they actually are. Investigate which magnifies more—big drops or little drops?

FUEL UP

sheet of newspaper with print showing
table
sheet of waxed paper
glass
water
straw
toothpick

BLAST OFF!

1. Spread the newspaper on the table.
2. Tear off a sheet of waxed paper about the size of a sheet of notebook paper.
3. Place the waxed paper on the newspaper.
4. Fill the glass half full of water.
5. Use the straw to transfer a few drops of water to the waxed paper. To do this, lower one end of the straw into the water, cover the other end with a fingertip, move the straw over the waxed paper, and lift off the fingertip just long enough to leave a few drops on the paper.
6. Use the toothpick to move a water drop over some print. Look at the print through the drop.
7. Move several other drops together to make one giant drop. Compare how the print looks through the giant drop and through the little drop.

BRAIN BOOSTER

Light usually travels in a straight line and at a set speed. However, light slows down as it passes from air into water. Because the surface of the drop was curved, light was also bent. The rounded shape of the drop bent the light outward. That caused the light to spread out, which made the image appear larger or magnified. A smaller water drop is a better magnifier than a large drop is. That's because its shape is more sharply curved.

BONUS PACK

Use the water-drop magnifier to take a closer look at things, such as a leaf's surface, the ridges on a fingertip, and cloth. To look at each object, carefully lift the waxed paper and set it on top of the area to be examined. Then place a fresh water drop on the paper at that spot and take a close look.

For More Science in a Minute Fun

Don't Try This at Home! Science Fun for Kids on the Go by Vicki Cobb (New York: Harper Trophy, 1999). A collection of more than 60 fun and easy science activities to do in all sorts of locations. Ages 9–12.

Entertaining Science Experiments with Everyday Objects by Martin Gardner (New York: Dover Publishers, 1981). Guided instructions that make it easy to investigate. Ages 8 and up.

Mr. Wizard's Supermarket Science by Don Herbert (New York: Random House Books for Young Readers, 2003). More than 100 super-simple experiments using items usually found in the supermarket. Ages 8 and up.

Projects for a Healthy Planet: Simple Environmental Experiments for Kids by Shar Levine (New York: John Wiley & Sons, 1992). Simple activities to help kids learn about the planet they live on and how they can help protect it. Ages 9–12.

Science in Seconds at the Beach: Exciting Experiments You Can Do in Ten Minutes or Less by Jean Potter (New York: John Wiley & Sons, 1998). Easy, quick experiments to do at the shore and in the backyard. Ages 9–12.

PART IV

Science Games

Challenge your senses and find out what makes each and every apple unique. Experience what it's like to be a seal trying to catch fish without becoming a shark's meal. Figure out the greatest possible number of ways to physically change a paper cup. Go fishing with a magnetic hook. Send marbles racing. And lots more! There's so much fun in each of these competitions that developing skills and discovering basic principles will just happen naturally. Let the games begin!

Biology Games

CHAPTER 10

Wonder Windows ③

Solve the puzzles and discover the features that are unique to birds, insects, spiders, fish, and mammals.

FUEL UP

old wildlife magazines (Be sure you have permission to cut out pictures.)

manila folders (or substitute large sheets of colored construction paper folded in half), one for each person

white glue

pencil

scissors

marking pen

BLAST OFF!

Have each family member follow these steps to prepare a Wonder Window Puzzle.

1. From a magazine, select and pull out a full-page color photo of an animal.

2. Open one folder and glue the animal's photo inside on the right-hand side. Below it, write what kind of animal it is, such as a bird.

3. Decide where to cut five windows in the left-hand page. These will be flaps that, when lifted, reveal just part of the animal's body. Plan to place a flap to reveal each of these parts:

   ● midbody to show the animal's covering, such as fur or feathers

- mouth

- eye

- feet

- tail (if there is one, or leg, if there isn't)

- any other part that would help identify what kind of animal this is, such as a bird's wing or a rabbit's ear

4. Use a pencil to mark the places to cut the flaps.

5. Have an adult use the scissors to make a U-shaped cut around each marked spot. The flap should be about 1-inch (2.5-cm) wide.

6. Fold and crease each flap so that it can be lifted easily.

7. Use the marking pen to number the flaps. Number them to reveal the least obvious clues about the animal first. Make the final flap reveal a body part that's most likely to give away the animal's identity.

8. Have family members exchange Wonder Window Puzzles and try to identify the hidden animals by opening the flaps in order.

9. Discuss how the animals were alike, such as having eyes and legs. Discuss how they were different, such as having feathers or fur.

10. Older children may want to identify a specific animal, such as a cardinal instead of simply a bird.

Brain Booster

Animals are divided into different groups that share similar characteristics, such as body structure. Knowing what key characteristics each animal group has makes it possible to identify these groups.

- Birds: covered with feathers, forelimbs are wings, mouth is surrounded by a beak or a bill, scales on their legs.

- Insect: hard outer body covering (exoskeleton), body is in three parts—head, thorax, abdomen—with antennae on head, six segmented legs.

- Spider: hard outer body covering (exoskeleton), body in two parts— combined head/thorax, abdomen—no antennae, eight segmented legs.

- Fish: covered with scales, fins, gills.

- Mammal: four limbs (may be legs or flippers and fins), have teeth, have hair (although it may be only a little); females have nipples to nurse young.

BONUS PACK

Have the family continue to build a library of Wonder Window Puzzles to share. The person constructing the puzzle should mark it with a colored dot, indicating the difficulty level: yellow for easy, blue for medium-hard, and red for the most challenging.

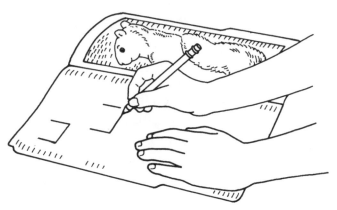

Find Your Apple ③

Explore how the senses of sight, smell, and touch provide information, while you discover that all living things—even apples—have their own unique **traits**, characteristics or features that can be used for identification.

FUEL UP

- 1 apple per player or team of players. Use only one variety of apple, such as Royal Gala, Red Delicious, or another variety. (You could substitute another type of fruit.)
- 1 pencil per player
- 1 sheet of notebook paper per player
- 3 more apples (or the substituted fruit)

BLAST OFF!

1. Give each player an apple, a pencil, and a sheet of paper.

2. Have each player draw lines to divide the paper into three columns labeled "sight," "smell," and "touch."

3. Have each player observe his or her apple using only eyes, noses, and fingers.

4. Have each player write a list of words telling what he or she observed from using the sense of sight in the "sight" column.

5. Repeat, having each player record what he or she observed using the senses of smell and touch.

6. Collect the fruit from each player. Place all the fruit together on a table and mix with the additional pieces of fruit.

7. Challenge the players to find their apples and explain how they know which one is theirs.

8. Wash and eat the apples.

Brain Booster

The players were probably able to pick their original apples out of the bunch because even though the apples looked, tasted, and felt very much the same, they each had some unique features. These may have been the color pattern on the skin, the shape, or something else. The human body has special parts that specifically collect information from the environment and send it to the brain. When the brain analyzes that information (which happens almost instantly), the person becomes aware of what is seen, heard, smelled, tasted, or felt. Eyes make it possible to see black and white, color, and movement. Ears make it possible to hear sounds and whether something is loud or soft. Noses make it possible to smell scents. Tongues and noses work together to make it possible to taste flavors. All parts of the skin make it possible to feel soft, hard, rough, smooth, hot, cold, and pressure. By using all of these human investigative tools, it's possible to detect the slight differences that make each apple—and anything else—unique.

Bonus Pack

Play "Common Senses." Hold up one apple and have someone use the sense of sight to observe the apple and identify its color, such as red. Next, have all of the players put their sense of sight to work, searching one room, the whole house, or a specified area outdoors to locate additional items that are the same color as the apple. Finally, go through these steps again, but this time instruct players to use their sense of touch to collect something that feels like the apple.

Fruit Salad ③

Discover how traits can be used to sort and classify objects, while you play this game. Then put all of the fruit together to make a tasty fruit salad.

Start by explaining that **classifying** objects means to group them by the ways they are alike and different.

Fuel Up

½ cup raisins in a self-sealing plastic bag
½ cup canned crushed pineapple in a self-sealing plastic bag
1 apple

1 banana
sheet of paper
pencil

Blast Off!

1. Two people or two teams can play. On a sheet of paper, write the name of each player or each team.

2. During each turn, one player thinks of a trait or a special feature that can be used to divide all of the fruits that were provided into two groups—those that have the trait and those that don't. For example, divide by the color yellow. Another possibility is wrinkled. Then the player divides all of the fruits into the two groups and names the trait. This trait should be recorded under the player's name or under the team's name.

3. The next player to take a turn must think of a trait that has not been used before. Play continues until no one is able to think of any other traits that could be used to divide the fruits into two groups, those that have that trait and those that don't.

4. The winner is the player or the team that comes up with the most traits for classifying the fruits.

5. When you're done classifying, use all of the fruit to make a fruit salad. Dump the raisins and the crushed pineapple into a salad or mixing bowl. Have an adult wash, core, and chop the apple into bite-sized bits. Add this to the bowl. Peel and slice the banana and add it to the bowl. Stir, serve, and eat.

Brain Booster

There are many different kinds of plants and animals in the world. For years, scientists tried out different systems for organizing these living things into groups. Eventually, in the mid-1700s, a scientist named Carolus Linnaeus worked out the system for classifying animals and plants that is still used today. Every specific kind of plant or animal is identified as a species. Similar species belong to a group called a genus. For example, a Siberian tiger's species is *tigris* and a lion's species is *leo* but both belong to the genus group *Panthera*. So a Siberian tiger is classified as *Panthera tigris* and a lion is *Panthera leo*. There are also larger groups that split up animals and plants by even more general traits. For example, all animals are divided into two big groups based on whether they have or don't have backbones. All animals with backbones are called vertebrates and all those without backbones are called invertebrates.

BONUS PACK

Collect a set of objects to play "Mystery Match"—another version of the classifying game. During each turn, a player thinks of a trait to use to classify the objects. Then, without naming the trait, he or she divides the objects into two groups—those that have the trait and those that don't. The other players must guess what trait was used to classify the objects.

Cookie Contest ②

Investigate how to pick a winner using two kinds of observations: qualitative observations and quantitative observations. Start by explaining that **qualitative** observations collect information using the senses of sight, touch, smell, taste, and hearing. **Quantitative** observations collect information using special instruments, such as a ruler, a balance scale, and a thermometer.

Tell the players that it's okay to put these test samples into their mouth.

FUEL UP

a pen or a pencil for each player

ruler

a clean sheet of notebook paper for each player

1 cookie each of 3 different brands of packaged chocolate chip cookies for each player

kitchen scales

magnifying glass (optional)

BLAST OFF!

1. Have each player draw lines on his or her paper, dividing it into three columns.

2. Place one brand of cookie at the top of the first column on each player's sheet of paper. Have the player write the name of that brand below the cookie.

3. Distribute the second and third brands of cookies in the same way.

4. Each player will need to collect the following quantitative observations about each cookie and write them on the paper:

   • Diameter (distance across)

   • Weight in grams or ounces

5. Each player will need to collect the following qualitative observations about each cookie and write it on the paper:

- Description of the way the cookie looks. For example: bumpy, brown, toasted, and so forth. (If a magnifying glass is available, use it to take a closer look.)

- Description of the way the cookie smells. For example: sweet, nutty, chocolaty, and so forth.

- Description of the way the cookie feels to the touch. For example: hard, soft, crumbly, and so forth.

- Description of the way the cookie tastes. For example, sweet, burnt, chocolaty, and so forth.

6. Based on both the quantitative and the qualitative observations, each player should rank the cookies that he or she believes should be the family's first, second, and third choice to purchase.

Brain Booster

The group's quantitative observations were probably more similar than their qualitative observations were. However, taste was probably the most important factor in making the decision of which cookie to purchase. Sight is the most commonly used sense. Almost a third of the human brain is devoted to analyzing the messages received from the eyes to let people "see." Touch sensors are found all over the body, but some body parts, such as the fingertips, have a lot more than other parts, such as the buttocks. Human noses have special smell sensors, but humans have fewer of these than many other animals, such as dogs. Still, people are capable of detecting a wide range of scents. The human taste-sensing organ, the tongue, has sensors capable of observing only sweet, sour, bitter, and salty flavors. Additional flavor observations come from these tastes being influenced by the scent of what reaches the mouth. Human ears have special sensors that detect vibrations moving as waves through gases (such as air), liquids, or solids. When the brain analyzes the messages from these sensors people "hear" sounds. People are capable of hearing a whole range of sounds but cannot hear sounds as high or as low as some animals can. For example, a dog's ear can pick up much higher-pitched sounds than the human ear can detect. And as people get older, they usually lose the ability to hear higher-pitched sounds.

While the human senses provide many qualitative observations about the world, these are often not precise enough to be scientific. Tools, such as a ruler, scales, and a thermometer, have been invented to supplement observations made by the senses. These tools provide quantitative information about the size, the weight, and the temperature of things in the world.

BONUS PACK

Let each player take a turn playing "Name That Cookie." Give each player another cookie from one of the sample bags. Then challenge people to identify the mystery cookie's brand, based on comparing it to the observations they made earlier.

Where in the World? ③

Introduce the world's different habitats, or places where groups of animals live, with easy-to-make jigsaw puzzles.

FUEL UP

> scissors
> old magazines (Be sure to have an adult's permission to cut out pictures.) or paper and colored pencils
> reference books (optional; use if drawing the pictures)
> white glue
> poster board
> pencil
> at least 6 colors of marking pens or crayons
> 6 sandwich-sized self-sealing plastic bags

BLAST OFF!

Have each family member follow these steps to prepare a "Where in the World?" puzzle.

1. Using scissors, each person should cut out a full-page or nearly full-page magazine photo of one of the following habitats: desert, rainforest, arctic tundra, meadow, freshwater, or ocean. Or draw and color a picture of one habitat. Use reference books as a guide for how the habitat should look.

2. Glue each picture on the poster board.

3. After about 15 minutes or when the glue is dry, cut around the outside edge of each picture so that you're left with separate pictures, each mounted on poster board.

4. On the back of each piece of poster board, draw lines to divide the picture into 8 to 12 puzzle pieces. Make the pieces interesting but simple shapes.

5. Make a colored dot on the back of each puzzle piece. Use the same color on all of the pieces for one puzzle. For example, mark all the pieces of the desert puzzle with a brown dot.

6. Put the puzzle pieces in a self-sealing plastic bag.

7. Exchange puzzles and have each player assemble his or her habitat.

BRAIN BOOSTER

All animals and plants have specific needs to survive. Their habitats have to provide them with food, water, shelter, and a place to raise their offspring. The plants and the animals in each habitat have special adaptations for living there. For example, polar bears have a thick layer of fat and a double layer of fur to keep them warm in their arctic habitat. And kangaroo rats dig underground burrows, in which they can escape the heat of their desert habitat.

BONUS PACK

Mix two or more habitat puzzles together. Then figure out how to separate and assemble the puzzles, based on the visible habitat clues. When in doubt about whether a puzzle piece belongs to one habitat or another, players can check by looking at the color code on the back.

Fill Your Plate ②

Get the scoop on what to eat for a well-balanced diet, while you play this gin rummy–style game.

FUEL UP

a marking pen (If you are drawing and coloring pictures of fruits and vegetables, you'll want several different colors of pens, such as red, yellow, and green.)

4 paper plates

54 3-by-5-inch (7.5-by-12.5-cm) index cards, or paper cut to this size

old magazines (Be sure you have an adult's permission to cut up the magazines.)

scissors

glue

BLAST OFF!

Get ready to play by preparing the following materials.

1. Use a marking pen to draw lines dividing each plate into 4 sections. Label the sections: 4 Vegetable and Fruit, 4 Bread and Cereal, 3 Milk, 2 Meat.

2. Label 16 cards with names of vegetables or fruit, such as bananas, carrots, peas, oranges, and so forth. If possible, find pictures of these foods in old magazines to cut out and glue onto the cards above or below each name. If you can't find pictures, you can draw them. Leave the other side of each card blank.

3. Label 16 cards with names of foods that are made from grains, such as cornbread, whole wheat bread, macaroni, oatmeal cookies, and so forth. Glue or draw pictures of these foods on the cards above or below each name. Leave the other side of each card blank.

4. Label 12 cards with names of foods that are made from milk, such as ice cream, cheese, cottage cheese, milk, and so forth. Glue or draw pictures of these foods on the cards above or below each name. Leave the other side of each card blank.

5. Label 8 cards with names of foods in the meat group, including beans, eggs, hamburger, tuna, turkey, and so forth. Glue or draw pictures of these foods on the cards above or below each name. Leave the other side of each card blank.

6. Label 2 cards "wild cards."

Play: The goal of each player is to collect 4 Vegetable and Fruit cards, 4 Bread and Cereal cards, 3 Milk cards, and 2 Meat cards to fill his or her plate.

1. Give each player a plate. If there are more than four players, divide the group into teams.

2. Put all of the cards together and shuffle the deck.

3. Deal 4 cards to each player. Put the rest of the stack, name side down, on the table.

4. Start to play by having the dealer turn over the top card on the stack and put it face up on the table.

5. The person to the right of the dealer then has first choice at either picking up this exposed card, drawing a card from the deck, or picking one card—sight unseen—from the player on his or her right.

6. Next, the player must dispose of a card either by putting it on his or her plate or by putting it—face up—on the discard pile.

7. Play continues until someone fills his or her plate with one day's well-balanced diet.

8. The 2 Wild Cards can be used in place of a card in any of the food sections.

9. If the deck has been completely turned over before anyone wins, shuffle the discard pile, turn it face down, and expose the top card. Then resume play.

BRAIN BOOSTER

Eating four servings from the vegetable and fruit group, four servings from the bread and cereal group, three servings from the milk group, and two servings from the meat group helps to ensure that you get the right proportion of fats, vitamins, carbohydrates, minerals, and proteins. Humans need these foods because

Carbohydrates supply the body with energy to be active.

Proteins help the body to build, maintain, and repair its tissues.

Fats provide stored energy to maintain a normal body temperature and keep hair and skin healthy.

Vitamins and minerals help the body to function properly.

BONUS PACK

Whip up these tasty pita pockets, which contain ingredients from all of the food groups. You'll need the following ingredients for each person: plate, pita pocket bread, 1 tablespoon of tomato paste, dash of dried oregano, sprinkle of salt and pepper, ½ of an all-meat hot dog sliced into pennies, 2 tablespoons of grated mozzarella or other cheese.

To prepare, carefully open the pita pocket. Mix the oregano, salt, and pepper with the tomato paste and spread it inside the pita pocket. Tuck in the sliced hot dog and grated cheese. Heat it on a plate in the microwave for 1 minute or until the cheese starts to melt. Enjoy!

Build a Food Chain ②

Hopscotch has been a popular game since the days of the Roman Empire. Give it a new twist and discover how a **food chain** functions. *Food chain* is the term used to describe food energy being passed form the green plants that produced it through a series of consumers.

FUEL UP

flat, paved area
chalk
permanent marking pen
8 3-by-5-inch (7.5-by-12.5-cm) index cards
tape
8 paper cups
something to use as a place holder, such as a small rock
bowl of popped corn

BLAST OFF!

This can be played alone or with a group.

1. Go outdoors to a flat, paved area, such as a sidewalk.

2. Use the chalk to draw a hopscotch court with 8 squares. The court should show boxes big enough to stand in with both feet. Arrange the boxes this way:

   1 single box

   1 single box

   2 boxes side by side

1 single box

2 boxes side by side

1 single box

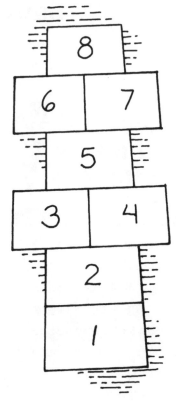

3. Number the chalk boxes 1 through 8. The boxes represent the parts of a food chain. Use the marking pen to print the following labels on the index cards.

    1—Green plant

    2—Plant eater

    3—Meat eater

    4—Bigger meat eater

    5—Even bigger meat eater

    6—Biggest meat eater

    7—Scavenger

    8—Rot

4. Tape one index card to the side of each cup.

5. Players alternate turns. Each player must progress through the court, one square at a time.

6. A player starts each turn by tossing the place holder (a small rock) into the square he or she wants to land in. During the player's first turn, the rock would be tossed into square 1. Then the player hops to square 1 and lands in it on both feet. The player picks up the rock and hops out again. Then the player collects a kernel of popped corn and drops it into the green plant cup.

7. During the next turn, the player proceeds to square 2 the same way.

8. When reaching two squares that are side by side, the player must land with a foot in each square, thus reaching both levels of the food chain. Then the player collects two kernels of popcorn—one for each level of the food chain.

9. If a player misses when tossing the rock into a square, he or she loses a turn.

10. If a player doesn't land inside a box on both feet, or if one foot is touching a line, he or she must repeat going to that square during the next turn.

11. The winner is the first player to make it all the way through the food chain, filling the cups.

12. Winners and losers munch their way through the food chain, sharing the popcorn in the cups.

BRAIN BOOSTER

A food chain is energy that is produced and then passed on in sequence through **consumers**, the life forms that eat the food that was produced. Green plants are the **producers**, the living things that make food energy. The first-level consumers are animals that only eat plants. Then these animals are eaten by other animals, the **predators**, the animals that catch other animals in order to eat them. Bigger, faster, stronger, and more clever predators eat smaller, slower, weaker, and less clever predators. When the predators die, they are consumed by yet other animals, the **scavengers**, the animals that eat dead animals. Finally, other living things—often tiny microbes—break down all dead matter, while consuming their share of the energy. Since energy is passed on through the chain, if something happens to one part of the food chain, this affects the other parts above that point. For example, if a blight wiped out dandelions, any insect that only ate dandelions would be in trouble. Then any bird that ate only the insects that ate dandelions would be in trouble, too, and so on. Luckily, in real life food webs are more numerous than food chains are. This means that while some animals specialize in one kind of food, most eat a variety of food items. For example, wolves eat lemmings, rabbits, caribou, and deer. In fact, they eat almost anything they can catch and kill.

THAT'S AMAZING

Blue whales are the largest animals on Earth, but they mainly eat tiny krill, shrimplike animals that live in large schools or groups. It takes lots of krill to make a blue whale's meal—as much as 8,000 pounds (3,600 kg) a day!

BONUS PACK

Play again. Before play begins, though, draw a line across square 6. Explain that due to loss of habitat, there has been a sharp drop in the population of those animals. After one person lands on square 6, draw a second line to cross out that square. Explain that the population is now extinct—all gone. Discuss what this means for the food chain. Continue to play, but draw a line across square 3. After 3 more turns, cross out square 3 because the population at that level is now extinct. Discuss what this means to the food chain.

Finders Keepers ③

Have fun exploring how some animals are able to find their mates or offspring in a group of hundreds or even thousands.

Fuel Up

12 3-by-5-inch (7.5-by-12.5-cm) index cards
red pen
blue pen
whistle
gummy fish

Blast Off!

Get ready to play by preparing the following materials.

1. Count out 6 cards that will become the Mom Set. Use the red pen to write one of these sounds on each card: toot, peep, ugh, eek, oops, rivet.

2. Now, create a second set of 6 cards to become the Baby Set. Use the blue pen to write one of these sounds on each of these cards: toot, peep, ugh, oops, rivet, and giggle. You'll notice that you're missing a match for Mom's "eek" and that there isn't a match for Baby's "giggle." As you'll discover during play, this is on purpose.

Play.

1. If you have more than 12 players, prepare more pairs of cards by making up additional sounds. If you have fewer than 12 players, just be sure to give more players cards from the Baby Set than from the Mom Set.

2. Divide the players into two teams. Don't worry if the teams aren't even.

3. Give each player on the first team a card from the Mom Set and a gummy fish. Give each player on the other team a card from the Baby Set.

4. Tell the players on the Mom team that they are mother Adelie penguins bringing food back to their hungry chicks. Explain that for each Mom to be sure that her chick survives, she must feed only her own chick.

5. Tell the players on the Baby team that they are very hungry. They need to find their own Moms in order to eat.

6. Explain to both groups that the way they will find each other is by making a special sound—the one written on each person's card.

7. Use the whistle to signal the beginning of play. When the Moms find the Babies, they should feed the chicks the gummy fish.

8. Discuss what happened. Consider what is likely to happen to any Baby, such as Baby Giggle, that doesn't find its Mom.

BRAIN BOOSTER

Some animals use sounds to locate their mates or their babies. For example, all Adelie penguin chicks look very much alike—fat, fuzzy, and gray—and there may be thousands of penguins in a breeding colony. When a parent penguin comes back from the sea with food, it needs to find its own chick to feed. This game is a fun way to see how the penguin's sound communication system works. It also demonstrates that sometimes a parent penguin doesn't return, for one reason or another. Then that penguin's chick is not likely to survive.

BONUS PACK

Collect the cards for each set and shuffle. Pass out new cards to each team. Play again, allowing just 1 minute for Moms and Babies to find each other.

Sharks and Seals ③

Get exercise and have fun while you investigate how the predator-and-prey relationship affects populations in a habitat. This game is best played by at least 20 people.

FUEL UP

paved surface or grassy area
chalk or a stake
at least 20 pebbles
whistle

BLAST OFF!

Get ready to play.

1. Create a playing court. If you're playing on a paved surface, such as an outdoor basketball area, draw a chalk line to mark each end. Leave an area about 30 feet (9 m) long in the middle. If you're playing on a grassy area, drive a stake into the ground to mark each end of the court. These are the shallow-water lines.

2. Scatter half the pebbles just beyond each end line. The pebbles are fish.

Play the game.

1. This game is played like rounds of tag.

2. One person is the shark ("It"). While moving, this person must hold his or her arms together above the head, creating the shark's big characteristic fin.

3. Everyone else is a seal.

4. The goal for the seals is to collect a fish (pebble) from the opposite end of the court and make it back to their starting shallow-water line. Seals cannot be tagged when they are beyond either shallow-water line.

5. The goal for the shark is to tag as many seals as possible.

6. Each tagged seal must stop moving and stand still until the end of the round.

7. For each round, divide up the seals so that about half are standing at either end of the court. Whistle to signal the start of play. Seals must immediately move toward the opposite shallow-water line. Once they pick up a fish, seals must return to their own shallow-water line, carrying their fish. Then they must drop their fish and go after another one.

8. After several minutes, whistle to stop the play. Any seal that collected at least one fish and is still "alive" will remain a seal in the next round. Each of those seals can also pick one of the dead seals to return to life as its offspring. All of the other dead seals become sharks in the next round. During any round, if a shark doesn't get any seals, it "dies" and is out of the game until the end of the set of rounds being played.

9. Play three rounds. Then observe what has happened to the seal and shark populations.

10. Play three more rounds. Then take another look at the seal and shark populations.

Brain Booster

Within every habitat, there are predators and prey. Predators are animals that must catch and eat other animals to survive. Prey are the animals that predators catch and eat. A prey population increases to the level that its food supply will support. As the prey population increases, predators are able to catch more prey, and the predator population increases. When there are large numbers of predators, they cause the prey population to decrease. Then, with less food available, the predator population decreases, and the cycle begins all over again.

BONUS PACK

Play "Sharks and Seals" again, adding one human fisherman (wearing a cap) whose goal is to tag sharks. How does this new hunter affect the wild predator population and the prey population?

Animal Splits ③

Win this game by learning to recognize key features that are unique to different animals.

FUEL UP

> 24 3-by-5-inch (7.5-by-12.5-cm) index cards
> colored markers or pencils

BLAST OFF!

Get ready to play by preparing the following materials.

1. Divide the cards into two stacks of 12 cards.

2. Create pairs of cards by writing the following words on the cards in each stack. Use the same color for each pair. For example, write "Elephant's" and "Trunk" in red. If possible, add a photo or a drawing to each card.

STACK 1	STACK 2
Elephant's	Trunk
Turtle's	Shell
Tiger's	Stripes
Rabbit's	Ears
Owl's	Eyes
Giraffe's	Neck

To play:

1. Put the two stacks together, making sure all of the cards are blank side up.

2. Shuffle.

3. Spread the cards, blank side up, in rows on a table.

4. The player who is taking the first turn begins by flipping over two cards. If the cards show the animal and its unique feature, the player collects the pair. Then the player continues, switching over another two cards. A player's turn ends when he or she fails to make a match.

5. When the cards do not make a pair, the player turns them over again so that they are blank side up.

6. The game continues, player by player, until all of the animals have been connected to their unique features. The winner is the player with the most pairs.

BRAIN BOOSTER

An animal's habitat, or the place where it lives, contains the food, the water, and the shelter it needs to survive. But animals have also developed special physical features that enable them to find or catch food, survive on the amount of water that is available, and make use of particular parts of the habitat for their shelter. An elephant's trunk helps it to collect food from high places and smell in all directions. A turtle's shell is a portable shelter. A tiger's stripes help it to blend in with the shadows, where it sneaks up on prey. A rabbit's ears help it to listen for predators so that it has time to escape. An owl's eyes help it to see prey from a distance, even in dim light. A giraffe's long neck helps it to reach leaves high up in the trees—too high for most other plant eaters to reach.

BONUS PACK

Add on to the deck. Decide together which animals and unique features to add. Some possibilities are: Alligator's Jaws, Frog's Legs, Woodpecker's Beak, and Camel's Hump. Discuss how each unique feature helps the animal be a success.

Animal Charades 1

Have fun discovering the features that make animals unique, while you role-play being those animals.

FUEL UP

2 pencils
15 slips of scrap paper
bowl

BLAST OFF!

1. Divide the family into two teams.

2. Write each of the following animals' names on a slip of paper: elephant, giraffe, shark, owl, and frog.

3. Tell the two teams the five animals that have already been named. Have each team think up five more animals that have unique features, and write each name on a slip of paper.

4. Fold all of the slips in half to hide the writing. Put the slips in a bowl and mix.

5. Have the teams take turns playing. During each turn, a different team member is "The Mystery Animal." A turn begins by the Mystery Animal picking one slip from the bowl. Next, the team members put their heads together for 1 minute to decide which feature will reveal that animal's identity. Then the player who is the Mystery Animal silently pretends to be that animal, and the other team guesses what it is.

6. Each team that has its Mystery Animal identified on the first guess gets 2 points. Any team that has its Mystery Animal identified within three more guesses gets 1 point. No points are scored after four tries. The animal's identity is then revealed.

7. Play continues until every team member on both teams has had a chance to be the Mystery Animal. If there are more than 15 players, have each team think up more than 5 animals or return the slips to the bowl and keep on playing.

8. When play is completed, the winning team is the one with the most points.

Brain Booster

All animals have some special feature, such as their size—big or small—their senses, or something else that can identify them. Those unique features, such as an elephant's trunk or an owl's big eyes, usually give them an advantage so that they can survive in conditions that don't suit other animals or help them to be successful when they're competing for food with other animals in their habitat.

Bonus Pack

Play again but have each team make up a set composed of Mystery Animals that all live in the same habitat, such as the desert or the ocean. This introduces different animals' adaptations for surviving in similar environmental conditions.

Gotcha!

Have fun discovering why predators have two forward-facing eyes.

FUEL UP

scissors
plastic milk jugs (1 per player)
markers
sheets of newspaper (at least 3 per player)
masking tape (optional)
chalk or string
scarf to use as a blindfold (one per player)

BLAST OFF!

1. To make the predators, ask an adult to use scissors to cut the side opposite the handle out of the milk jug. This forms a scoop with a handle.

2. Use the markers to give each predator a face with an open mouth.

3. To make the prey, wad up each sheet of newspaper into a tight ball. If necessary, secure with tape.

4. Outdoors, use chalk or string to form the "hunting line" on pavement or grass.

5. Have an adult put the blindfold on each player so that it covers just the right eye.

6. Each player should hold his or her predator by the handle and stand behind the hunting line.

7. Have an adult toss the prey, one at a time, toward one or another of the players.

8. Players must catch the prey with the predator.

9. Players score one point for each prey that's caught. Play at least 3 rounds, announcing a winner for each round.

10. Have players remove their blindfolds and repeat the action.

11. Discuss which way it was easier to catch prey—when using only one eye or using both eyes.

BRAIN BOOSTER

Each eye supplies the brain with slightly different images. The brain analyzes both sets of visual messages to create **depth perception**, the ability to judge the distance to something. Knowing how far away something is makes it easier for you to hit a target. It also lets predators judge where to pounce to catch prey. That's why animal predators, such as wolves, tigers, and hawks, have two forward-facing eyes.

BONUS PACK

To help a toddler start to develop his or her depth perception, create this ball game. Start by screwing an eye hook into a Ping-Pong ball or a small rubber ball. Tie one end of a 2-foot (0.6-m) piece of string to the ball and the other end to a rubber band. Or use a 2-foot (0.6-m) piece of narrow elastic. Attach the string so that the ball hangs just high enough for the toddler to bat the ball with one hand.

Hide a Critter ③

Explore how animals use **camouflage**, or the ability to blend in with their surroundings, to escape becoming a predator's lunch.

FUEL UP

Each player will need the following materials:
    scissors
    a sheet of white paper
    crayons
    a pencil
    tape
    optional materials (cotton balls, glue, glitter, toilet paper tubes, pipe cleaners, and a
        ball of modeling clay)

BLAST OFF!

1. Assign each player a different "habitat" (a specific area indoors or outside). Challenge players to create an imaginary animal that is so well camouflaged, it can't be found by "predators" (the other players) during a 30-second search.

2. Distribute the materials and allow a set time period, such as 20 minutes, for each player to create his or her camouflaged critter. You may

also supply other optional materials for players to use in creating their critters. Provide separate working places so that each player can keep secret his or her critter's camouflaged features.

3. Have all of the players leave the area where the camouflaged critters will be hidden. Then, before returning, allow time for each player to be alone to hide his or her critter.

4. While all of the other "predators" watch, assign one to search the habitat for the camouflaged critter. Assign a different "predator" to search each habitat.

5. The winners are all the kids who created critters that weren't found. Discuss why those critters were successful camouflage artists. Brainstorm different ways that the losers (kids who created critters that were found) could improve their critters' camouflage.

Brain Booster

Animals have special coloring and body structures to help them avoid being seen in their natural habitats. This helps a prey animal hide from predators. For example, a snowshoe hare has a brown summer coat to help it hide among tall grass. Then, as winter approaches, the hare sheds its brown hair and grows a white coat that's just right for hiding in plain sight in the snow. But predators may also be camouflaged to help them sneak up on prey. For example, a lion's tawny-colored coat is just the right color to let this hunter slip through tall grass until it's close enough to pounce on its prey.

That's Amazing

Chameleons change color to stay camouflaged when they move from one place to another. A chameleon can change color because its skin has a layer of special color-filled cells. The chameleon's brain controls whether these cells expand or shrink, revealing more or less of the coloring matter. And a chameleon can make its colorful switch in as little as 20 seconds!

Bonus Pack

Use the critters to play another version of this game. Give a player one of the critters to hide where its features will provide camouflage. Have one player be the "predator" and cover his or her eyes while the critter is being hidden. Then have the predator search for its prey while the other players call out "warmer" or "cooler" as clues.

Habitat Safari ③

Discover how a local habitat, such as a forest, a field, a park, or even your own backyard, supplies what animals need to live there.

Fuel Up

notebook
camera (optional)

Blast Off!

1. Do this as a single group or make it a challenge between two family teams.

2. Choose a habitat and plan a field trip there with your notebook. (Be sure to stay on public property, and be sure an adult goes with you.)

3. Find places in the habitat that supply each of these things that animals need to survive. Write about and sketch or photograph what you find.

   ● water supply

   ● food for a plant-eating animal

   ● food for a meat-eating animal

   ● shelter where an animal could escape predators and/or bad weather

   ● a place where an animal could raise its young

4. Also find as many creatures as possible that are living in the habitat, such as insects, spiders, birds, mice, frogs, earthworms, snails, and others. If you don't spot the creatures, look for signs that they are there, such as silvery snail trails on a sidewalk, animal tracks on bare dirt, holes in a leaf where an insect munched a meal, and a bird's nest in a tree's branches. Make notes on the animal or its signs, and draw or photograph them for your notebook.

Brain Booster

To live in a habitat, animals need a supply of water, enough of the kind of food they eat, shelter from the weather and from predators, and a safe place to raise their young. Different kinds of animals have different needs, so a variety of animals can share the same habitat without competing with each other. For example, to raise their young, birds like sheltered spots on branches for their nests; owls prefer the tops of dead trees or hollow cavities in trees; rabbits raise their young under plants or in holes under rocks; and insect youngsters grow up on leaves or in water—even in puddles.

BONUS PACK

Take your toddler on his or her first habitat safari. Guide the young explorer to experience this habitat by letting the child touch everything that is safe to feel, such as rough tree bark, velvety flower petals, crumbly dirt, and more. Watch for animals that live in this habitat. For a variation on this scavenger hunt, take your child searching for colors in nature.

Walk the Plank ③

In this activity, youngsters have fun developing motor skills and balance.

FUEL UP

A 5- to 6-foot (1.5- to 1.8-m) length of a 2-by-4-inch (5-by-10-cm) board (or substitute a strip of cardboard)

BLAST OFF!

1. Outdoors, place the board or the strip of cardboard on the grass. Or, indoors, place the cardboard on a level floor.
2. Take turns walking along this plank without stepping off.
3. Each player should move in a different way during each crossing. Start with these and add others:

> little steps
>
> big steps
>
> forward two steps, backward one step, repeat
>
> walk backward
>
> walk with arms outstretched
>
> walk with arms crossed over chest

BRAIN BOOSTER

This activity lets players develop control over large muscles and improve their use of sensory information about the body's position to stay balanced. A person's ability to keep his or her body balanced (steady and level) depends on the brain analyzing and responding to information that's received from three different sources: the eyes, the muscles and the joints, and the inner ears. Especially important are the messages received from the neck, which reveal the direction that the head is turned. Messages from the ankles are important, too, indicating the movement of the body in relation to the floor. Messages from the ankles also reveal whether the body is moving across hard, soft, bumpy, or smooth terrain. Special areas in the inner ear called the semicircular canals send the brain messages about whether the head is steady, tipped, or moving.

BONUS PACK

Play "Twist and Shout." Pick a grassy area outdoors, away from obstacles, and place a goal, such as a milk jug, somewhere in the area. Have players stand so that they won't bump into each other. When one player says "Go," all players should spin around three times, then run to the goal. When the player shouts "Stop!" the player closest to the goal is the winner. This game is more challenging than it sounds because the brain is tricked for an instant after the body stops spinning, so it's hard for the body to balance and head straight for the goal. What happens is that the fluid in the ears' semicircular canals keeps on moving and sends confusing signals to the brain.

CHAPTER 11

Chemistry Games

Mad Matter

Develop a winning strategy while you investigate the states of matter.

FUEL UP

31 3-by-5-inch (7.5-by-12.5-cm) index cards
marker pens

BLAST OFF!

1. Get ready to play by preparing the following materials.

2. Divide the cards into two stacks.

3. Use the markers to write the following information on the cards in each stack

MATTER STACK	SAMPLE STACK
Gas	Inside inflated balloon
Gas	Air
Liquid	Water
Solid	Ice
Gas	Exhaust from car
Liquid	Gasoline
Solid	Wood
Solid	Nail
Gas	Steam

MATTER STACK	SAMPLE STACK
Liquid	Milk
Solid	Gold ring
Solid	Rock
Liquid	Paint inside a can
Liquid	Pancake syrup
Solid	Sugar

3. Write a master list showing the cards in the Matter Stack and their pairs in the Sample Stack, as shown above.

4. Use the marking pens to draw a wizard on the last card. Label it "Mad Matter."

To play:

1. The goal is to collect as many pairs as possible and not to end up with the Mad Matter. This game is designed for two players. To have more players, add 10 pairs of cards per player.

2. Put the two stacks together, add the Mad Matter card, and shuffle the deck.

3. Deal five cards to each player.

4. Put the remaining cards, face down, on the table. Turn over the top card and lay it beside this stack.

5. Play begins with the person to the right of the dealer. During each turn, the player may first pick one card from the stack—either the one that's face down on the stack or the top card that's face up. Or the player may select one card from the hand of the person on his or her left.

6. During a player's turn, that person also lays down any pairs he or she is holding. A pair is a match between the Matter card and a Sample card, such as "Solid" and "Wood." If in doubt, check the master list.

7. A player's turn ends when the player takes new cards from the face-down stack to replace any that were used to form pairs.

8. The game ends whenever a player is able to use up all of his or her cards to make pairs.

9. Players, except for anyone holding the Mad Matter card, get one point for each pair they made during the game. The person with the Mad Matter card scores no points for that game.

10. Play one game or a series of games until one player scores 50 points.

BRAIN BOOSTER

Matter is made up of tiny building blocks called molecules. The molecules in a specific kind of matter, such as water, all have the same structure. All matter exists in one of three states: solid, liquid, or gas. Matter can change its state and still remain whatever kind of matter it is. For example, water is usually a liquid, but it can be a gas (steam) or a solid (ice).

BONUS PACK

Role-play being each state of matter. Have all the family members stand as close together as possible to be solid. Tell them to move about two steps apart and start wiggling around to be liquid. Then they should move at least five steps apart or as far apart as possible and do jumping jacks to be gas.

Amazing Matter ②

Discover the secret of how to draw mazes. Then continue to explore the three states of matter.

FUEL UP

For each maze:
    pencil
    2 sheets of plain white paper
    colored pencils
    ruler
    envelope

BLAST OFF!

Prepare to play. Have family members work individually or in teams to prepare a maze.

1. Follow these steps to draw a maze on the paper.

    ● Draw a box that fills the paper, leaving an opening at one corner to be an entrance into the maze. Also leave an opening at the corner of the box opposite the entrance to be an exit.

    ● Use a colored pencil to draw a line that touches one edge of the box and only one edge. The line can be straight, angled, or curved, or it can have several bends in it.

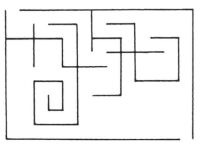

- Draw a second line that touches any point on this first line. It can be straight or curved or can have bends.

  - Draw a third line that touches the one you just drew. Again, it can be straight, curved, or with bends. It may even cross the second line where it touches that line, but it must *not* touch or cross any other line.

  - Continue adding lines to make the maze as complex as you like. Begin with each new line touching any other line, but the new line must never touch any line other than the one where it originated.

2. Find the path that lets a player move through the maze from the entrance to the exit. Along this path, write the names of things that are one state of matter, such as solids. These could include a car, a sidewalk, bread, and an eggshell.

3. At other places in the maze, write the names of things that are the other states of matter, in this case, liquids, such as water, milk, and soda, or gases, such as air, steam, and exhaust fumes.

4. At the top of the maze, write the kind of matter that is the key to successfully solving the Amazing Matter maze.

5. On the second sheet, list the items, in order, that can be found along the correct pathway through the maze. Fold this and put it into the envelope. Do not seal the envelope.

Play

1. Exchange mazes and solve the puzzles.

2. To make it possible for more than one person to solve each puzzle, have each players use a finger to trace the path, rather than drawing a line.

BRAIN BOOSTER

Each state of matter has its own special traits.

Gas: The molecules move around quickly and are spaced far apart. A gas does not have its own shape or volume but fills up any container that it's in.

Liquid: The molecules move about more slowly than those of a gas, slipping past each other. A liquid has its own volume, but it does not have a shape. It takes the shape of the container it's in.

Solid: The molecules are packed tightly together—so tightly that they move very slowly or only vibrate in place. A solid has its own shape and volume.

BONUS PACK

Whip up a drink that contains all three states of matter. Scoop vanilla ice cream (solid) into a tall glass. Fill the glass half full of any fruit juice, such as orange juice (liquid). Add enough carbonated lemon-lime soft drink to finish filling the glass. The bubbles that add fizz to this drink are bubbles of carbon dioxide (gas).

Cup-er-oo ③

Divide everyone up for this lively family team challenge and discover what a physical change can and cannot do to a paper cup. Before starting, explain that a physical change is one that changes anything but the molecular structure of matter.

FUEL UP

Materials needed for each team:
    1 paper cup
    scissors
    crayon
    pencil and paper to keep score

BLAST OFF!

1. Divide into teams.

2. Brainstorm for 1 minute to think of all the physical changes that could be made to the paper cup. For example, cut a hole in it, tear it, wrinkle it, and color a design on it.

3. The teams take turns making one physical change to the cup. No team may repeat a change that has already been made. One person may want to act as referee and keep a list of all the physical changes that are made.

4. The winner is the team that's able to make the most physical changes to the cup.

BRAIN BOOSTER

There are two ways matter can be changed: a physical change and a chemical change. A **physical change** is any change that affects the matter's shape, size, and color but does not alter its molecular structure.

A **chemical change** alters the matter's molecular structure, making it into a different kind of matter.

Bonus Pack

Have the family teams face off again. This time, challenge the teams to use paper cups and any optional recycled materials to create physical changes that become a cup sculpture.

Cook Off

Make a game out of cooking up a chemical change. Then enjoy the results.

Fuel Up

Materials per team. These ingredients are enough to make about 10 pancakes.

   mixing bowl

   mixing spoon

   1 cup all-purpose flour

   1 teaspoon baking powder

   ¼ teaspoon salt

   1 tablespoon sugar

   1 egg

   1 cup milk

   2 tablespoons vegetable oil

   ½ cup any of the following optional fruits: bananas, raisins, apples, blueberries, pineapple, strawberries

   1 teaspoon any of the following flavoring options: vanilla, cinnamon, chocolate, caramel, maple syrup

   large skillet or griddle

   butter or margarine

   maple-flavored syrup or powdered sugar

   spatula

Blast Off!

1. Divide into family groups.

2. Each team chooses which of the optional ingredients to add to the basic mix.

3. Each team prepares its pancake mix, observing how the ingredients change when combined.

4. Have an adult add 1 tablespoon of butter or margarine to the skillet or griddle. Heat until just hot.

5. Have an adult cook each team's pancakes, using ¼ cup of batter per pancake.

6. Cook until bubbly. Flip and cook until golden brown on both sides.

7. Eat to compare the results. A panel of judges could vote for a winner.

8. Discuss how the pancakes are different from any one of the original ingredients.

Brain Booster

In a chemical change the molecular structure of the matter changes to form new matter. Bubbles, fizzing, and smoking are often signs that this is happening. Heating matter is one way that chemical changes can happen.

Bonus Pack

Make a family cookbook, showing recipes that are the family's favorite chemical changes. Make copies to share with grandparents, aunts, and uncles.

CHAPTER 12

Physics Games

Quiz-O-Gram ②

Investigate how an electric circuit works, while you build and play this game.

FUEL UP

scissors
poster board
hole punch
marking pen
transparent tape
aluminum foil
D-cell battery
flashlight bulb

BLAST OFF!

Make the game.

1. Using scissors, cut a piece of the poster board about the size of a sheet of notebook paper.

2. Use the punch to make 5 holes in a line down one long side of the poster board.

3. Make 5 holes along the opposite side of the poster board that line up with the first set of holes.

4. Make up a list of things to match, such as animals and what the baby of each kind of animal is called: frog—tadpole; shark—pup; elephant—calf; bear—cub; fish—fry.

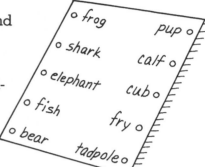

5. Write the names of the animals next to the holes on the left-hand side of the poster board.

6. Write the names given to the babies next to the holes on the right-hand side of the poster board, but mix them up. For example, opposite "frog," put "fry," and opposite "bear," put "pup."

7. On the back, tape aluminum foil strips—shiny side down—connecting the hole next to the animal with the hole next to the correct name given to its baby. For example, tape a strip connecting the hole next to "frog" with the hole next to "tadpole." Don't worry if the strips cross over each other. Be sure the foil completely covers the holes.

8. Trim off any aluminum foil that extends beyond the edge of the poster board.

9. Cut out one more strip of aluminum foil. Tape one end over the knob end of the D-cell battery.

Play.

1. Set the D-cell battery, flat end down, on the hole next to the first animal name.

2. Wrap the free end of the foil strip leading to the battery around the screw base of the flashlight bulb.

3. Touch the tip of the bulb's base to the hole next to the possible correct answer.

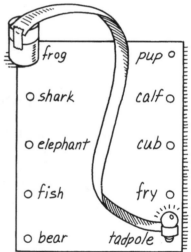

Brain Booster

The bulb lit up if you touched the correct answer. If the bulb didn't light, touch it to another answer hole until it does. That will reveal the correct answer. Electricity is made up of charged particles called electrons. Electrons are normally parts of atoms. Everything in the universe is made of atoms, but these building blocks are too tiny for your eyes to see. And electrons are even tinier. Sometimes, electrons are knocked out of their atoms. Then those loose electrons may bump into other atoms and free still more electrons.

When the electrons are flowing from one place to another, the charged particles form an electric current. Sometimes this current may flow through a pathway, such as a wire. Then the electricity is said to flow in a circuit. When the electricity flows from a source, through a pathway, and back to that source, the circuit is called a complete circuit. When you touched the correct answer in the Quiz-O-Gram, the circuit was completed so the bulb lit up.

BONUS PACK

Have the family work in teams to prepare different Quiz-O-Grams. Then exchange these and tackle the challenge of finding the correct answers. Continue to build a library of Quiz-O-Gram cards. These cards make learning fun and are perfect for a family game night or a rainy day.

Go Fishing ③

Find out what kind of materials a magnet will attract, while you play this game.

FUEL UP

refrigerator magnet (magnet on a card or another shape)
sturdy tape, such as duct tape
scissors
sturdy paper plate
hole punch
a 3-foot (0.9-m) piece of sturdy string or twine
paper towel tube

BLAST OFF!

1. Tape the refrigerator magnet to the center of the paper plate.
2. Using scissors, cut a hook shape out of the plate that is slightly larger than the refrigerator magnet.
3. Punch a hole in the top of the hook.
4. Tie the string through the hole in the hook.
5. Tie the free end of the string to one end of the cardboard tube. Wrap the string around the tube until the string hangs down about halfway to the floor.
6. Go fishing by moving the magnet hook close to a "fish" (an object that you think might be attracted to the magnet). A fish is caught when it sticks to the magnet. *Note: Even though this is a weak magnet, do not get it close to a watch or a computer.*
7. Whenever a fish is caught, observe what kind of material that fish is made of.

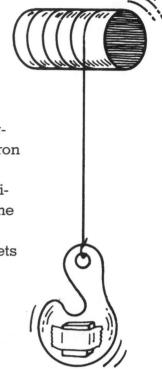

8. Release each catch by gently pulling the magnet away from the fish.

9. Try to catch as many different kinds of fish as possible.

Brain Booster

Only certain kinds of materials could be caught by the magnet. A magnet is something able to attract, or pull toward itself, objects made of iron or steel. Magnets are created when the atoms (building blocks of the matter) are made to line up in orderly rows. Quite a few types of materials will become at least slightly magnetic, but iron and steel become the strongest magnets. Because of the way the atoms are arranged, magnets are said to have two poles—a north pole and a south pole. Magnets attract objects made out of iron and steel. A magnet's power to attract extends beyond itself in an area called its force field.

Bonus Pack

Do the magnet push. Remove the bar magnets from two refrigerator magnets. Propel one magnet across a smooth, flat surface using the force field of a second magnet (note that only one side of each magnet will push on the other magnet; the other sides will attract). If two like poles are brought close together, the reaction is that the magnetic fields will push apart. If two unlike poles are brought close together, the magnetic fields pull the magnets together.

Shadow Says  ③

Go outdoors on a sunny day to get the family energized, as you investigate shadows.

Fuel Up

flat area, such as a cement driveway, where shadows show up clearly

Blast Off!

1. Everyone should spread out to avoid blocking another person's shadow.

2. Take turns being the "Shadow," the person who challenges everyone else.

3. Play the game as you would "Simon Says." Players should obey only the commands that begin with the words "Shadow says."

4. All action instructions should involve the player and his or her shadow, such as

   ● Shadow says stand with your shadow in front of you.

   ● Shadow says touch your shadow.

   ● Shadow says make your shadow wiggle.

   ● Shadow says make your shadow shrink.

   ● Shadow says make your shadow stretch.

   ● Shadow says jump on your shadow.

5. Any player who performs an action that doesn't begin with "Shadow says" is out for the remainder of that game.

6. The winner is the last person still in the game.

BRAIN BOOSTER

Light travels in a straight line. Light directed at an object causes a shadow to appear opposite the light source. The shadow is the area where light is blocked from reaching the surface. Outdoors, the sun is the light source. Because Earth turns, the sun's position in the sky changes during the day. For this reason, shadows created by sunlight striking objects—or people—change during the day.

THAT'S AMAZING

Groundhog Day is an ancient holiday that celebrates the shadow. Its origin is an old German event called Candlemas Day, celebrated on February 2, the midpoint between winter and spring. On that day, a lighted candle was placed in every home and the day's weather was checked. According to superstition, if the sun came out on that day, the weather would remain wintry for six more weeks. In Germany, people watched the badger to see whether sunshine would allow this animal to see its shadow. When German settlers arrived in North America, people changed this tradition to checking whether a groundhog could see its shadow.

BONUS PACK

Make a monster shadow—a creature made up of shadow shapes cast by every member of the family standing close together in a group. Make as many different shadow monsters as possible this way.

Flashlight Tag

Discover that light travels in a straight line, while you play this classic game.

FUEL UP

grassy or open area outdoors without obstacles
1 flashlight

BLAST OFF!

1. Go outdoors on a clear, dark night.

2. At a signal to start, all of the players but one will run away from a starting point.

3. The remaining player is "It" and will have the flashlight.

4. After counting to 20, "It" will switch on the flashlight.

5. "It" tries to tag a player by shining the flashlight beam on his or her chest.

6. As soon as a player is tagged, he or she takes the flashlight and becomes "It."

7. The player who was just "It" cannot be tagged by the new "It." So he or she is "Free" until the next time the flashlight changes hands.

8. After everyone plays for a little while, discuss strategies that players can use to avoid being tagged, such as standing behind a tree and turning sharply as "It" tries to aim the flashlight's beam. Discuss why these strategies work—the reasons are that light travels in a straight line and can't pass through a solid object.

Brain Booster

Light is made of particles of energy, called photons, which travel in waves. Light waves travel in straight lines. When light strikes something, it is absorbed, passed on, or reflected.

Bonus Pack

Each player will need a flashlight, or the group can be divided up into small teams with flashlights. Each player or team needs to be told a code to flash, such as one short, one long, and one short. Another player or team should be given the same flashing code. The players will stand in a tight cluster with their backs together. Then the players or teams will run away from each other while they count out loud to 10. At that moment, each player or team should begin to flash the code, then quickly move toward any other player or team flashing the same code. The winners are the first players or teams to unite with their partners.

Marble Racetrack ②

Investigate how momentum can be put to good use, while you develop problem-solving skills. The goal is to make the marble travel as far as possible without stopping.

Fuel Up

at least 5 paper towel tubes (or substitute poster board that's rolled and taped into long tubes)

masking tape

marble

scissors

measuring tape

Blast Off!

1. Work together as a team. Or double the supplies and let two teams challenge each other. Use a tape measure to measure how far the marble travels each time it is launched.

2. Connect two tubes together with tape to see if the marble will go all the way through them. Launch the marble into one end of the long

tube with a single snap of an
index finger. To do that, place the
tip of the index finger's nail
against the thumb and move the
finger forward quickly.

3. Keep adding on tubes until the
    marble stops before it reaches the
    end of the last tube in the racetrack.

4. Design a way to make the marble gain momentum (speed and
    energy) and travel farther.

5. Try elevating the early part of the racetrack so that the marble
    runs downhill.

6. Try cutting one of the tubes into
    small pieces and taping these
    together to make a bend in
    the racetrack. Then put
    something under this part of
    the track to add a second
    elevated section, making the
    marble run downhill again.

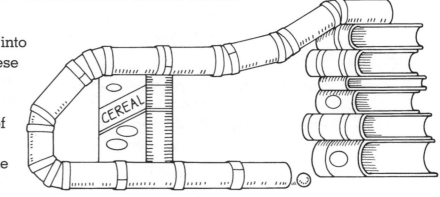

Brain Booster

As the marble rolled, friction (rubbing against the surface) made the
marble lose a little energy with each roll. Gravity also made the marble
lose a little energy. But momentum helped to keep the marble moving.
Momentum is the effect of the object's mass and speed on its movement.
Flicking the marble gave it energy to start it rolling. Having the marble
roll downhill made it pick up speed and gain momentum. Lifting up parts
of the racetrack also gave the marble an energy boost to keep it rolling.

Bonus Pack

Just for fun, discover that momentum can be passed on from one to
another in a group of objects—or even in a group of people. Have family
members sit on the floor in a line and squeeze close enough together to
put their legs on either side of the person in front of them. Have the person at the front of the line lean back, gently shoving the person behind
him or her backward. This motion will pass through the group, causing
the person at the end of the line to flop backward.

For More Science Games Fun

Bet You Can! Science Possibilities to Fool You by Vicki Cobb and Kathy Darling (New York: HarperCollins Juvenile Books, 1989). With the help of science, kids will successfully accomplish challenges and learn about the human body, matter, and energy. Ages 9–12.

Bouncing Eggs: Amazing Science Activities You Can Do at Home by William R. Wellnitz (Monterey, Calif.: McGraw-Hill/Contemporary Books, 1999). Investigating science mysteries around the house. Ages 9–12.

Games, Puzzles, and Toys: Hands-On Science Activity Projects from the Smithsonian Institution by Simms Taback (Milwaukee, Wis.: Gareth Stevens, 1993). Science activities that families can share to have fun discovering. Ages 9–12.

How to Really Fool Yourself: Illusions for All Your Senses by Vicki Cobb (New York: John Wiley & Sons, 1999). This book is a blend of humor, science, and hands-on activities that trick the senses. Ages 8 and up.

Sandbox Scientist: Real Science Activities for Little Kids by Mary Anne Lloyd (Chicago: Chicago Review Press, 1995). Science play using easy-to-find materials. Ages 4–8.

The Kids' Science Book: Creative Experience for Hands-On Fun by Robert Hirschfeld (Charlotte, Vt.: Williamson Publishing, 1995). Experiments and games that are science in action. Ages 8 and up.

PART V
Science Toys

Build and launch a toy rocket. Create a toy submarine. Make a pioneer doll out of cornhusks. Whip up two kinds of play clay, including one that you can eat. And lots more! Building and operating toys is a fun way to discover science.

CHAPTER 13

Biology Toys

Test Eye-Hand Coordination and Make a Ball and Cup Toy ②

Discover a toy that has been popular for hundreds of years—the ball and cup.

Fuel Up

    screw eye
    a rubber ball small enough to fit easily into a paper cup
    18-inch (45-cm) piece of sturdy string
    masking tape
    sturdy paper cup
    paint-stirring stick
    duct tape

Blast Off!

1. Twist the screw eye into the rubber ball.

2. Tie one end of the string to the screw eye.

3. Use a loop of masking tape to attach the bottom of the cup to the larger end of the stick.

4. Have an adult use duct tape to anchor the cup to the stick.

5. Tie the free end of the string to the stick just below the cup. Anchor with tape.

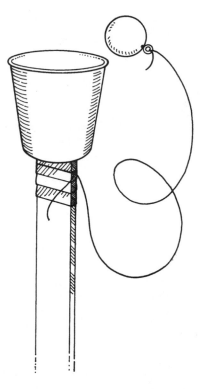

6. Holding onto the stick's handle, move the cup and ball to launch the cup into the air.

7. While the ball is in the air, move the cup to catch it.

Brain Booster

Eye and hand coordination is the ability to control your hand movements in response to what your eyes see, in order to do a task. It's a learned skill that you develop with practice. This ability is important to help you accomplish a lot of tasks, such as writing, coloring between the lines, cutting something out of paper, and tossing a ball to hit a target. The ball and cup toy is a fun way to develop eye and hand coordination. This toy has been popular around the world for centuries. The Japanese play with a similar toy, which has a ball with a hole in it, attached to a stick with three cups and a pointed end. In addition to catching the ball in one after another of the cups, the ultimate goal is to catch the ball with the pointed end of the stick.

Bonus Pack

Now challenge each family member to catch the ball in the cup as many times in a row as possible. Determine the family champ and schedule periodic rematches.

Make a Cornhusk Doll ②

Make a doll the way the pioneers did, while you think about the features that make it look human.

Fuel Up

newspapers

large mixing bowl

water

10 dried cornhusks (Pull husks off ears of corn on the cob and dry them on newspapers, or purchase corn husks that are used to prepare tamales.)

scissors

yarn

black marking pen (fine tip)

10-inch (25-cm) square of cloth

BLAST OFF!

1. Cover the work area with newspapers.

2. Fill the bowl nearly full of warm tap water.

3. Place 9 unbroken cornhusks in the water and soak until soft (about 10 minutes).

4. To make the hair, cut 6 pieces of yarn, each 4 inches (10 cm) long.

5. Place 5 pieces of yarn side by side in a bundle. Use the other piece to tie this bundle in the middle. Trim close to the knot.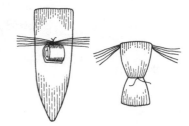

6. Select one cornhusk to make stuffing for the doll's head. Fold in the edges of the cornhusk. Next fold up the pointed end. Then roll up the husk.

7. To finish the head, place another husk—ridged side up—on the table. Lay the rolled-up husk about halfway down this. Set the hair bundle just above this, with the yarn sticking out on either side. Fold the flat husk over the hair and the rolled-up husk, and use yarn to tie tightly around the "neck."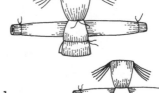

8. Roll up another husk lengthwise to form the arms. Tie yarn tightly around either end at the "wrists."

9. Slide the arms under the flap of husk below the doll's neck. Tie yarn around the "chest" to hold the arms in place.

10. Finish the doll's body by placing whole husks—narrow end toward the head—on the front and the back.

11. While you hold the husks in place, have a partner tie yarn around the doll's "waist."

12. Use the marking pen to give the doll a face.

13. Fold the cloth in half lengthwise, wrap this shawl around the doll's neck, and cross the ends over the doll's chest. Tie on a yarn belt to secure the shawl.

14. Observe how the doll's body is like a human's.

BRAIN BOOSTER

A doll is one of the world's oldest kinds of toys. The goal has always been to make them as lifelike as possible, so dolls' bodies have bilateral symmetry, meaning that the left side is nearly identical to the right.

Dolls found in graves of ancient Egyptians, Greeks, and Romans were molded from clay or carved from wood or ivory.

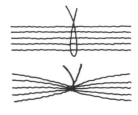

Dolls were also made from materials like cornhusks and rags. Later, dolls were given jointed bodies so that they could mimic how people move. Doll makers then tried to make dolls with more lifelike features. To do that, they made dolls' heads out of painted china or wax. In the late 1940s, even more realistic dolls were created from molded plastic and vinyl. They were given "rooted" hair instead of glued-on wigs.

Bonus Pack

Find out just how similar a human's two halves are. Compare left and right hands and feet, eyes and ears, teeth, and even the way hair grows on the left and the right sides of the head. Consider how it helps to have two nearly identical halves. Brainstorm how it might be useful to have one side uniquely different from the other and what features it might be handy to have.

Make a Stethoscope ③

Discover how this instrument amplifies sounds, as you explore how a doctor uses it.

Fuel Up

    scissors
    clean, empty half-gallon (2-l) plastic bottle
    18 inches (45 cm) of rubber or vinyl tubing that will fit easily through the mouth of the
        bottle (available at stores that sell plumbing or aquarium supplies)
    modeling clay
    duct tape

Blast Off!

1. Have an adult cut the top off the bottle about 2 inches (5 cm) below the neck to create a funnel.

2. Thread the vinyl tubing through the bottle's mouth so that the end is just inside the neck.

3. As you hold the tube in place, have a partner pack modeling clay up through the funnel end into the neck around the tubing. (Be sure that none gets in the tubing.)

4. Wrap duct tape around the bottle's mouth and the tubing.

5. Listen through the tube as a partner holds the funnel end of the stethoscope against his or her chest.

6. Have the partner move the funnel around until the heartbeat sounds are loudest.

7. After the partner has been sitting quietly for at least a minute, count the number of heartbeats in 30 seconds. Have your partner do 10 jumping jacks, then use the stethoscope to count the number of heartbeats in 30 seconds immediately after he or she stops.

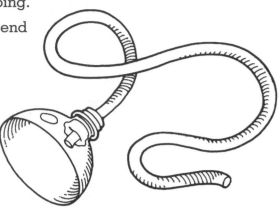

BRAIN BOOSTER

For you to hear, sound waves have to enter the ear, where they cause the eardrum to vibrate. Then those vibrations are transmitted by a series of three small bones to sensors that detect the vibrations and send signals to the brain. The sound waves created by the human heartbeat are faint by the time they pass through the body's bones and muscles. The stethoscope helps to collect those sound waves and deliver them directly into the ear. A real stethoscope has two tubes—one for each ear. This helps to ensure that the listener hears the heartbeats, instead of other noises. A doctor also uses a stethoscope to listen to a person's lungs to make sure the breathing sounds are normal.

In 1816, Dr. Rene Laennec invented the stethoscope by listening to a patient's chest through a paper tube. Before that time, a doctor listened by pressing his or her ear to the patient's chest. Today, some stethoscopes have electronic parts that amplify sounds as much as 100 times.

THAT'S AMAZING

Your heart rate increases during and after a meal. The shortest distance the heart pumps blood is to itself. The longest distance it pumps blood is to the toes—a trip that takes the blood almost a minute.

BONUS PACK

Compare the heartbeats of children and adults. If possible, listen to a pet's heartbeats to see how the animal's heart rate compares to a human's.

Make a Spinning Disk Toy to Trick Your Eyes ③

With this entertaining toy, discover something special about how the eyes and the brain work together to let people see.

FUEL UP

juice glass
sturdy paper plate
pencil
scissors
hole punch
blue and orange markers or crayons
3-foot (0.9-m) piece of sturdy string

BLAST OFF!

1. Put the drinking glass on the flat part of the plate and use the pencil to draw around its base to make a circle.

2. Cut out the circle, creating a paper disk.

3. Use the pencil to draw a line straight across the middle of the disk.

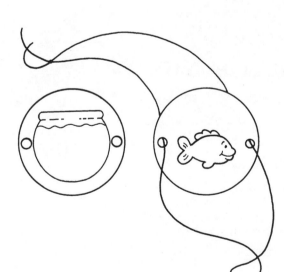

4. Punch two holes opposite each other and near the edges of the disk.

5. Draw the outline of a fish bowl so that it nearly fills the circle inside the holes. Press down hard so that the imprint shows on the back. Color the fish bowl blue, as if it's full of water.

6. On the opposite side of the disk, draw and color a goldfish that fits inside the outline of the fish bowl (but do not draw the outline).

7. Thread the string through each hole. Bring the ends together and tie a knot.

8. Slide the disk to the center of the string loop.

9. Hold one end of the loop in each hand so that the disk hangs down.

10. Flip the disk over again and again, twisting the string.

11. When the string is tightly twisted, lift the disk to eye level and pull the ends of the string apart. Watch the spinning disk to see the illusion.

Brain Booster

You saw the fish inside the fish bowl. This "trick" is really a result of what happens normally to let people see. When light reflected from an object strikes light-sensitive cells at the back of the eyes, these cells send signals to the brain. But the light-sensitive cells retain an image for about one-fifth of a second before sending a new signal. For a fraction of a second, the brain may still be getting messages about an image that has changed. This phenomenon, called **persistence of vision**, is the reason the image of the fish bowl and the fish appeared to be combined when the disk was spinning. The brain was mentally bridging the two rapidly appearing images. Dr. J. A. Paris invented this spinning disk toy in 1827. He named it a thaumatrope (pronounced tho-ma-trohp), for the Greek word meaning "wonder turner."

Bonus Pack

Construct other spinning disks to make a smile appear on a blank face, apples appear in an empty basket, or a bird appear inside a cage.

CHAPTER 14

Chemistry Toys

Mix Up Two Kinds of Clay ①

Investigate how combining chemicals can produce something with characteristics that are different from those of the individual ingredients.

FUEL UP

For each type of clay:
    clean mixing bowl
    clean mixing spoon

For Peanut Butter Clay:
    1 cup creamy peanut butter
    1½ cups powdered milk
    3 tablespoons honey

For Salt Clay:
    1 cup plain (not self-rising) flour
    ½ cup salt
    ½ cup hot water
    1 tablespoon vegetable oil

BLAST OFF!

For Peanut Butter Clay (If you keep all of the work surfaces and your hands clean, this clay can be eaten.)

1. Mix the ingredients together until smooth.

2. If the clay is too stiff, add more honey. If it is too gooey, add more powdered milk.

For Salt Clay (Do not eat the Salt Clay.)

1. Pour the dry ingredients into a bowl and mix.

2. Add the hot water and mix again. Add the oil and mix until well blended.

Brain Booster

Chemical changes happen when the molecules of two or more kinds of matter join together to make something new. It's not like making a salad, where the individual ingredients maintain their own unique characteristics and can be picked out separately. A chemical change is like baking a cake, where the ingredients combine to produce something new and different. Experiment with each clay to see how they are different from the original ingredients. These differences will include how flexible they are and how well each is able to hold a shape.

Bonus Pack

Cover a work area with clean waxed paper. Use the Peanut Butter Clay to make edible sculptures. Add pretzels, raisins, coconut, and other food items. Sculptures made from the Salt Clay can air dry until they are hard. These can be painted with acrylic paints and sealed with craft varnish. Both kinds of clay can be stored in airtight containers in the refrigerator for about a week.

Launch a Toy Rocket ②

Use a chemical reaction to power up this easy-to-make model rocket.

Fuel Up

scissors
white plastic grocery or garbage bag
transparent tape
plastic film canister with a snap-on lid
safety goggles
Alka-Seltzer tablet (or other bicarbonate of soda tablet)
rock
water

BLAST OFF!

1. Use the scissors to cut off a strip of plastic from the plastic bag that is about an inch (2.5 cm) wide and 6 inches (15 cm) long.

2. Tape one end of the plastic to the inside of the film canister's lid.

3. Now go outdoors. Put on the safety goggles and hit the Alka-Seltzer tablet once with the rock to break it into pieces.

4. Put about half of the broken tablet pieces inside the film canister.

5. Fold up the plastic strip so that it's tucked flat against the inside of the film canister's lid.

6. Set the bottom of the film canister on a flat surface, clear of any objects or people.

7. Add 1 tablespoon of water to the canister, then quickly snap the lid on the canister and walk at least 10 steps away.

8. Watch the toy rocket launch.

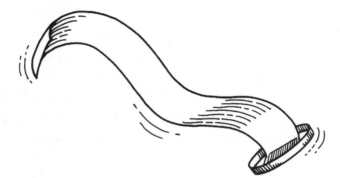

BRAIN BOOSTER

An Alka-Seltzer tablet is made out of baking soda, powdered citric acid, and a little aspirin. The aspirin didn't have any effect on this experiment. Baking soda is a kind of chemical called a base. When bases and acids combine, they react. When water is added, the acid and the baking soda dissolve and start to react with each other, producing carbon dioxide gas. The film canister only looked empty, but, in fact, it was really full of air, so there wasn't much room for the carbon dioxide gas. The gas built up inside the can until it pushed the cap off with explosive force. That sent the lid flying into the air, pulling the plastic streamer with it.

BONUS PACK

Test to find out what is the smallest amount of an Alka-Seltzer tablet that you can use to launch the lid.

Make a Magic Bottle ③

Some liquids are thicker, or denser, than others. Make this toy to explore what happens when two liquids of different densities meet.

Fuel Up

a clean, empty small clear plastic bottle with a screw-on lid
rubbing alcohol (isopropyl alcohol)
blue food coloring
clear vegetable oil
3 tablespoons glitter
other small, lightweight colorful items, such as colored beads
duct tape

Blast Off!

1. Remove the bottle's label.

2. Fill the bottle about one-fourth full of rubbing alcohol.

3. Add enough food coloring to make the rubbing alcohol bright blue.

4. Slowly pour in the vegetable oil until the bottle is full almost to the rim.

5. The vegetable oil is denser (heavier) than the alcohol, so watch as it sinks below the blue alcohol.

6. Pour in the glitter and any other items.

7. Add enough vegetable oil to completely fill the bottle to the rim.

8. Put the lid on tight and wrap the cap with duct tape to seal it.

9. Lay the bottle on its side and roll it to see the action. Tip it upside down for an instant and watch what happens when you tip it back again. Shake the bottle, then watch what happens.

Brain Booster

Rolling, tipping, and shaking broke down the particles of the heavier liquid and forced them to be suspended in the lighter liquid. However, the particles of the denser liquid soon began to stick together again, and the two liquids quickly separated. A

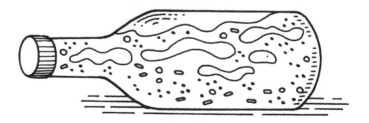

substance's density is the measurement of its mass (how much matter it contains and how much space it takes up) compared to its volume (the three dimensional space it's in). Bubbles formed as the less dense liquid, alcohol, rose to the top again. The glitter and the other items were all different densities, or weights. Those that were denser than the oil settled to the bottom of the bottle. Those of about the same density as the oil floated in the oil. Those that were about the same density as the alcohol floated in the alcohol. And those that were less dense than the alcohol floated to the top of the bottle.

Bonus Pack

Perform the activity "Stick Oil and Vinegar Together" (see page 31) to learn how to make two liquids of different densities blend and stay mixed.

CHAPTER 15

Physics Toys

Make a Top ③

Build your own top and find out what's needed to keep this toy spinning for the longest possible time.

FUEL UP

2 pencils, one sharpened and one not sharpened
2 sturdy paper plates
transparent tape
modeling clay

BLAST OFF!

1. Use the sharpened pencil to mark the center of each paper plate.

2. Have an adult use the pencil point to poke a hole through each plate's center mark. Widen the hole enough to push the pencil through easily, but not so wide that it slips through.

3. Thread the unsharpened pencil—eraser end last—through the bottom of one plate.

4. Slide the second plate—bottom down—onto the pencil.

5. Tape the edges of the plates together.

6. Slide the plates down the pencil until they are about 2 inches (5 cm) above the eraser.

7. Shape a walnut-sized lump of clay and press this around the pencil just above the plates.

8. Set the eraser end of the pencil on a smooth, hard surface. Holding the pencil at the end opposite the eraser, roll the pencil between your fingers and let it go to start the top spinning.

9. Count one thousand one, one thousand two, and so forth, to time how long the top spins.

10. Repeat, giving the pencil a sharp twist to make the top spin faster.

BRAIN BOOSTER

A top spins because twisting it provides energy to set it in motion. Then momentum, the fact that something spinning tends to keep on spinning in its same position, keeps it going. With each spin, though, the top experiences friction as it pushes through the air, and this friction uses up a little energy. This makes the top slow down a bit with each spin. Eventually, the top revolves slowly enough that it topples over and stops.

THAT'S AMAZING

According to the Guinness Book of World Records, on December 18, 1998, Hall Graham set the top-spinning record at Woodstock High School in Georgia. His top spun for 2 hours, 52 minutes, and 11 seconds before it toppled.

BONUS PACK

Remove the clay from around the pencil. Then add weights around the edges of the top by taping pennies all around the rim of the top plate. Try out the top again to find out if this makes the top spin longer. Brainstorm anything else that might increase how long the top spins. Check with an adult to make sure the ideas are safe to do and then try them. Each family member could build his or her own top and compete to see whose top spins longest.

Play Partner Puller ②

Investigate how pulling something apart can exert enough force to power up a flying saucer—or, in this case, a flying cup.

FUEL UP

scissors
sturdy paper cup
colored markers
2 6-foot (2-m) pieces of sturdy string, such as packaging twine
4 toilet paper tubes

Blast Off!

1. Using scissors, cut the bottom out of the cup, making it a tube.

2. Use the markers to make a colorful design all over the cup.

3. Have an adult use the scissors points to poke three equally spaced holes around the middle of the cup.

4. Snip outward from each hole to make a "V" shape. Fold each "V" up to form a fin that will catch the air.

5. Thread both pieces of string through the middle of the cup.

6. Tie the end of each string to a separate toilet paper tube to create a handle for each end of the string and make it easier to hold onto.

7. Lay the strings side by side on the ground or the floor, with the cup in the center.

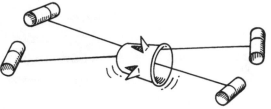

8. Have one partner pick up one set of handles. Have the other partner pick up the other set.

9. Have the partners move apart until the strings are stretched tight between them.

10. Partner 1 should hold his or her handles side by side, while Partner 2 pulls his or her handles—and the strings—apart to send the cup flying toward the opposite person.

11. As soon as the flying cup arrives, Partner 2 should put his or her handles together. Then Partner 1 should pull his or her handles apart, forcing the cup back toward Partner 2 again.

12. Repeat steps 10 and 11 to keep the cup traveling back and forth.

Brain Booster

This toy demonstrated one way that force can make something move. In this case, the force of pulling the strings apart forced the flying cup away.

Bonus Pack

Find out what happens if both partners pull their ends of the rope apart at the same time. Have someone time how fast the partners can send the flying cup on a complete trip.

Make a Super Bouncer ②

Explore what makes a ball bounce, while you make a ball.

FUEL UP

knife (for adult use only)
cork bottle stopper
lots of small rubber bands
yardstick (meter stick)

BLAST OFF!

1. Have an adult use the knife to shape the cork stopper into a round ball shape.

2. Wrap rubber bands—one at a time—around the cork ball, being careful to maintain the round shape. Continue until the cork is completely covered.

3. Tuck any loose rubber band ends into the ball.

4. Add 20 more rubber bands, being careful to space them evenly to maintain the ball's round shape.

5. Tuck in any loose ends.

6. Have a partner hold a yard stick (meter stick), with the zero end down, touching a flat, hard surface. Then drop the ball from the top of the measuring stick to see how high it will bounce. Do three test bounces to be sure the results would be likely every time. If the ball bounces higher than the measuring stick, mark the highest point it reaches with an outstretched arm. Have your partner measure the distance from the ground to that point.

7. Add 20 more rubber bands and test the ball again.

8. Repeat until adding rubber bands no longer increases how high the ball will bounce or until the ball is too fat to hold any more rubber bands.

THAT'S AMAZING

When a bat strikes a ball, it compresses the baseball to about half of its original diameter.

In the last 100 years, baseballs have changed in only one way. In 1974, cowhide replaced horsehide as the ball's covering. Otherwise, the ball remains exactly the same: a cork core inside a rubber ball, surrounded by nearly a quarter mile (0.4km) of woolen yarn, a winding of cotton/polyester yarn, and a leather jacket sealed with 108 stitches. The finished ball must weigh between 5 and 5.25 ounces (141 and 148 g) and be between 9 and 9.25 inches (22 and 24 cm) around.

Brain Booster

A ball bounces because it is made of a type of material that compresses (packs together under pressure) when it strikes a solid surface. As the material returns to its original shape, the ball pushes away from the surface and rebounds. That rebound is a bounce.

Bonus Pack

Brainstorm ways that you could improve the ball to make it bounce higher, such as changing the core or wrapping the core in cotton. Check with an adult to be sure your idea is safe to try. Then build a second ball and compare its bounce to that of the original.

Race Balloon-Powered Boats ②

Investigate the equal and opposite reaction that propels these boats forward. Then hold a family race with everyone competing to build the fastest boat on the water.

Fuel Up

quart-sized (liter-sized) milk carton
duct tape
marking pen
adult partner
scissors
rubber balloon
twist tie
bathtub or outdoor wading pool

Blast Off!

1. Close the spout end of the milk carton and tape it shut.
2. Draw a circle slightly smaller than a Ping-Pong ball in the middle of the carton's flat bottom.
3. Have an adult cut out this circle.
4. Insert the deflated balloon—closed end first—into the carton through the hole.

5. Inflate the balloon inside the carton. Twist the neck and tie with a twist tie to keep the air from escaping.

6. Fill the bathtub or a wading pool.

7. Set the carton boat on the water at one end of the tub or the pool, with the spout end aimed toward the opposite side.

8. Release the twist tie and watch the boat sail.

Brain Booster

When the balloon's neck was released, the air trapped inside rushed out. This air escaping out the back of the boat pushed the boat in the opposite direction—forward. This demonstrated a basic law of motion: For every action, there is an equal and opposite reaction.

Bonus Pack

Supply each family member with the same boat-building basics as identified in the "Fuel Up" section. Allow each person to brainstorm other materials—except for any kind of fuel-powered motor—that might make his or her boat travel faster. Before beginning construction, hold a family conference to be sure that each person's idea is safe to try. Then allow time for boat building and hold a family boat race.

Fly a Straw Plane ③

Discover how air flowing over a curved surface gives this model, as well as real planes, lift.

Fuel Up

scissors
sheet of white typing paper
ruler
transparent tape
1 plastic straw
measuring tape

Blast Off!

1. Using scissors, cut a strip of paper 1½ inches (3.75 cm) wide by 6 inches (15 cm) long.

2. Cut a second strip of paper 1½ inches (3.75 cm) wide by 8 inches (20 cm) long.

3. Use tape to hold the ends of the shorter strip together to form a loop.

4. Do the same thing with the longer strip.

5. Place the straw inside the smaller loop and slide the loop to one end of the straw. Tape it in place.

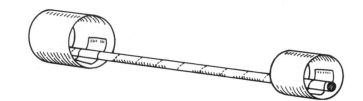

6. Do the same with the larger loop, taping it to the opposite end of the straw.

7. On a day when it is not windy, go outdoors and stand at a marked starting point.

8. Hold the plane by the straw, with the loops on top of the straw and the smaller loop aimed forward. Throw the plane forward.

9. Have a partner help you measure how far the plane flew.

10. Being careful to launch the plane the same way each time, fly the plane three more times. Then compute an average of how far the plane flew. *Note: To compute an average, add together the results of all of your tests and divide that total by the number of tests you made.*

Brain Booster

The straw plane and real planes fly because of **lift,** the force that happens when there is more air pressure below the wing than above it. The fact that the wing is curved on top and flat underneath causes the difference in air pressure. The same amount of air flows over both surfaces of the wing, but the air flows faster over the curved surface at the top of the paper loop. Fast-moving air exerts less pressure down on the wing than does the slow-moving air pushing up from below. The faster the plane travels, the greater this pressure difference, until the lift force becomes great enough to overcome the plane's weight. Then the plane flies. A real airplane's wing isn't a loop, but it's curved on top and flat below. So, like the paper plane, the airflow is faster over the upper surface of the wing. The smaller loop goes first because, being of a smaller diameter, it cuts through the air more easily than the bigger loop does. This helps to reduce the friction on the whole plane as it moves through the air.

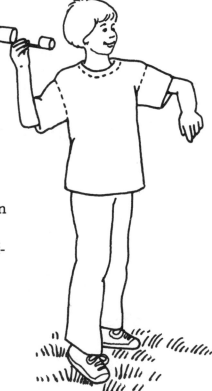

BONUS PACK

Brainstorm ways that you could modify the plane to make it fly even farther. Things to try could include making both loops large or small, throwing the large loop end forward, and adding weight to the nose.

Make a Parachute Jumper ②

As you play with this toy, discover how a parachute works to slow a jumper's fall.

FUEL UP

black permanent marking pen
cork bottle stopper
8-inch (20-cm) piece of wire, such as florists' wire
scissors
plastic trash bag
transparent tape
hole punch
4 16-inch (40-cm) pieces of sturdy string

BLAST OFF!

1. Use the marking pen to draw a face on the cork.

2. Fold the wire in half and stick the fold into the top—the head end—of the cork. This forms the jumper's two arms.

3. Cut a 12-inch (30-cm) square out of the plastic trash bag.

4. Cover all four corners of the piece of plastic with tape to reinforce them.

5. Use the hole punch to make a hole in each reinforced corner.

6. Thread one string through one corner and tie the string.

7. Repeat with the other three corners.

8. Fold the square in half lengthwise.

9. Bring the two strings on the left side together. Tie the ends.

10. Do the same thing with the two strings on the right side.

11. Bend one of the jumper's wire arms around one of the string loops. Twist to anchor it.

12. Bend the other wire arm around the free string loop and twist to anchor it.

13. To launch, hold the center of the plastic parachute, checking that the strings are straight.

14. Toss the parachute into the air or lift it up and drop it.

15. Watch the parachute jumper's descent.

BRAIN BOOSTER

The parachute trapped air, creating drag, or resistance to it moving through the air. This would slow the descent of anyone or anything suspended below the parachute. However, as the parachute moved through the air, it tended to create eddies of air on either side. That made the chute sway from side to side. When the parachute tipped enough, some air slipped out from under the parachute. That caused the parachute to drop faster and swing around.

BONUS PACK

Adding a vent in the parachute helps to keep the parachute from tipping to lose air. Try making a second identical parachute jumper but put a V-shaped flap or vent near the center top of the folded parachute. Compare how this parachute toy drops with the way the original drops. Which stays in the air for the longest time?

Make a Mini-Sub ②

Discover how a submarine submerges and surfaces again, as you make and operate this toy sub.

FUEL UP

tall glass
water
several foil packets of ketchup, soy sauce, or salad dressing
clean, empty half-gallon (2-l) plastic bottle with a screw-on lid

Blast Off!

1. Fill the glass with water. Drop in the packets one at a time. Choose the one that floats highest in the water. This will be the mini-sub.
2. Fill the bottle almost full of water.
3. Push the packet into the bottle.
4. Add more water so that the bottle is full to the rim.
5. Screw on the lid.
6. Squeeze the sides of the bottle to make the mini-sub sink.
7. Release the sides to let the mini-sub rise again.

Brain Booster

Turn an empty glass upside down, push it straight down into a sink full of water, then tip the glass. The air inside the glass will escape as bubbles. Because air is lighter than water, the bubbles will rise to the surface. An object is buoyant when the amount of water it pushes aside can support its weight. The packet was somewhat buoyant because it had an air bubble trapped inside. Squeezing the bottle increased the water pressure inside the bottle, so the water squeezed the packet, and the air bubble inside the packet became smaller. That made the packet slightly less buoyant. Then the mini-sub sank a little. Releasing the bottle decreased the water pressure, and the air bubble inside the packet expanded again. This made the packet more buoyant so that the mini-sub rose inside the bottle.

Bonus Pack

Find a small plastic ring, such as the plastic ring left around the neck of bottle when the cap is removed. Push this inside the bottle with the packet. Make the mini-sub rise and sink to maneuver it into a position where it touches this ring target.

Build a Bull Roarer ③

Discover how making air vibrate can be noisy.

Fuel Up

drill (for adult use only)
paint-stirring stick

3-foot (0.9-m) piece of sturdy string
metal washer
duct tape
colored markers

Blast Off!

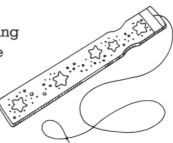

1. Have an adult drill a hole in the center of the handle of the stirring stick. The hole should be just large enough for the string to slide through easily.

2. Tie one end of the string to the washer to keep it from pulling through and put the other end of the string through the hole in the stick. Secure it with a piece of duct tape.

3. Decorate both sides of the stick with colorful designs.

4. Tie a loop at the free end of the string to use as a handle.

5. Find an area outdoors away from obstacles and people. Hold the string by the loop handle, and spin the stick around and around over your head. Listen to the sound the toy makes.

6. Be careful to reduce the bull roarer's speed slowly.

Brain Booster

This toy is called a bull roarer because of the sound it makes. The faster it swings, the louder the roar. Watch while someone else spins the bull roarer, and you'll see that the wood is actually spinning rapidly as it moves through the air. This spinning motion makes the air molecules vibrate. Sound is vibrating air, and, in this case, the vibrations create a humming noise. The bull roarer was one of the earliest kinds of musical instruments. The sound was thought to compare to the sound of the wind or even thunder.

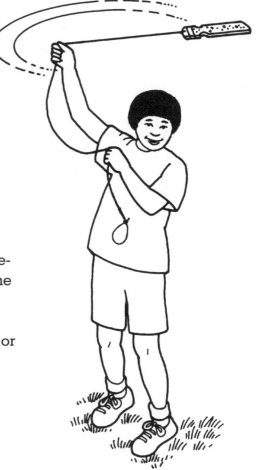

Bonus Pack

Try making bull roarers of three different lengths to see how that affects the tone they make.

Make a Squawking Can ③

Here's another way to discover that vibrating air creates sounds—sometimes sounds that are pretty weird.

FUEL UP

safety goggles
hammer and nail (for adult use only)
clean, empty metal can
12-inch (30-cm) piece of sturdy string
metal paper clip
masking tape
scissors
clean, thin sponge

BLAST OFF!

1. Have an adult put on the safety goggles and use the hammer and nail to punch a hole in the middle of the can's bottom.

2. Tie one end of the string to the paper clip.

3. Thread the free end of the string through the hole in the can from the inside to the outside so that the paper clip is inside the can.

4. Tape the paper clip to the can's bottom.

5. Using scissors, cut about a 2-inch (5-cm) wide strip off one end of the sponge.

6. Wet the sponge and squeeze out the excess water.

7. Hold the can in one hand so that the string is hanging down. Hold the piece of sponge between the thumb and the index finger of the other hand.

8. Pinch the string between the two sides of the damp sponge.

9. Slide the sponge down the string with either one long pull or a series of sharp jerks.

BRAIN BOOSTER

You heard a squawking or clucking sound. Pulling on the string moved the can bottom. Each time the can bottom moved, it vibrated the air inside the can. The vibrations traveled through the air to your ear, bumped against your eardrum, and triggered signals to be sent to your brain. As soon as your brain analyzed these signals, which happened almost instantly, you became aware of a sound.

BONUS PACK

Try making different squawking cans using bigger and smaller cans than the original one. Then listen to the sounds the cans make to discover that the bigger the can—and the bigger the column of vibrating air—the deeper the sound that's produced. The smaller the can—and the smaller the vibrating column of air—the higher the sound.

Make a Flute

Make your own flute and explore how it produces different tones. Then play a tune.

FUEL UP

scissors
1 plastic straw
knife (for adult use only)

BLAST OFF!

1. Using scissors, cut the end of the straw into a V-shape, with the point at the end of the straw.

2. Flatten the "V" with your thumbnail.

3. Have an adult use the knife's point to "drill" three holes in the straw: one in the center and the other two at equal distances on either side of the center hole.

4. Put the "V" between your lips and blow.

5. Next, cover the holes with your fingers and blow.

6. Repeat, blowing as you lift different fingers to uncover the holes one at a time, two at a time, and again all at once.

BRAIN BOOSTER

Blowing through the "V" forced air between the upper and lower pieces of plastic. That made the two plastic pieces vibrate (move back and forth rapidly). The vibrating plastic caused the air inside the straw to vibrate. The length of this vibrating column of air depends on how much air is inside before there's a hole where the air can escape. The longer the column of moving air is, the lower the sound that's produced.

Bonus Pack

Use the straw flute to play the song "Mary Had a Little Lamb," by following the pattern below. The highest-sounding note is number 1 and the lowest-sounding note is number 3. Produce high, low, and medium sounds in the following pattern to play this familiar song.

1, 2, 3, 2, 1, 1, 1

2, 2, 2, 1, 1, 1

1, 2, 3, 2, 1, 1, 1

1, 2, 2, 1, 2, 3

Make a Penny Orbit a Balloon ③

This toy is a fun introduction to **centrifugal force**, an action that propels something outward from a certain point.

Fuel Up

penny
large balloon

Blast Off!

1. Push the penny into the balloon through its mouth.

2. Have an adult blow up the balloon and tie the neck to seal it.

3. Hold the balloon and move it around and around to make the penny circle the inside of the balloon.

4. Make the penny keep going around the balloon while you count to 10.

5. Stop moving the balloon and watch the penny keep on going around.

Brain Booster

Moving the balloon applied centrifugal force to the penny and slung it away from the middle with each rotation. Because the penny was inside the balloon, it was trapped and couldn't keep moving away. So it **orbited**, or followed a particular path, around the inside of the balloon. When the balloon stopped moving, momentum (stored energy based on the penny's weight and the speed it was traveling) kept it going for an instant or two. The faster it traveled, the longer it continued to orbit. Then as the friction of rubbing against the balloon made the penny lose energy, it slowed down. Eventually, the coin was moving too slowly to keep on orbiting.

Bonus Pack

Fill a plastic bucket half full of something light, such as packing peanuts. Stand away from other people in a clear area, such as in the middle of an empty garage. Hold the bucket by the handle and quickly swing it in a circle over your head and down again. If this is done quickly enough, centrifugal force will sling the stuff inside the bucket away from you just long enough to keep it inside the upside-down bucket. If the weather is warm, have the family go outdoors in swimming gear and take turns trying this activity with a bucket of water.

Make a Whirlpool Bottle ②

Create a water toy to investigate centrifugal force, the action that moves molecules outward from a center point.

Fuel Up

    drill or hammer and nail (for adult use only)
    2 half-gallon (2-l) bottles with screw-on plastic caps
    duct tape
    scissors
    water
    red food coloring

Blast Off!

1. Have an adult drill a ½-inch (1-cm) hole through the center of each bottle cap. (If a drill isn't available, have the adult make a hole with a hammer and nail and then wiggle a scissors point in the hole to enlarge it.)

2. Set one cap—open end down—on top of the table.

3. Set the other cap—open end up—on top of the first cap, making sure the two holes line up.

4. Use duct tape to anchor the two caps tightly together. Trim off any tape that extends beyond the edge of the cap.

5. Working at a kitchen sink or outdoors, fill one bottle nearly full of water. Drip in enough food coloring to color the water bright red.

6. Screw the bottle cap onto the bottle that's full of water.

7. Have a partner hold onto the full bottle, while you turn the empty bottle upside down and screw it onto the other cap.

8. Turn the bottles over so that the full one is upside down on top. Watch what happens for a few seconds.

9. Quickly spin the bottles around as you count to five and watch what happens.

10. Turn the bottles over and give them another spin to keep the water tornado going.

Note: If a lot of water leaks from the caps, remove the tape, dry the plastic, and have an adult use adhesive glue for plastic to bond them together. This glue will need to dry overnight.

Brain Booster

When the bottle of water was just sitting still over the lower "empty" bottle, very little water dripped through the holes. When you spun the bottles around quickly to make the circling water move outward against the sides of the bottle, the water circled around the outside of the bottle. This outward motion is centrifugal force. The "empty" lower bottle also wasn't really empty. It was full of air. So when the water moved to the sides of the bottle and out of the way, the air rose up through the center of the water. And when the air got out of the way, the water was able to flow into the bottom bottle.

Bonus Pack

Experiment to find out what happens if one bottle is bigger than another. Pair up a quart (1-l) and a half-gallon (2-l) bottle.

Make a Kaleidoscope ②

Make reflections multiply with this intriguing toy.

FUEL UP

hammer and nail (for adult use only)

cardboard can with a snap-on lid, such as the kind that certain brands of potato chips come in

sandpaper

scissors

second identical snap-on lid

3 hand mirrors that will fit inside the cardboard tube. (Or cut strips of cardboard and glue shiny mylar onto one side of each strip. Mylar is available at stores that sell hobby supplies.)

masking tape

paper towel

pea-sized ball of modeling clay

colored tissue paper (or you can color thin paper with watercolor paint or markers)

BLAST OFF!

1. Have an adult use the hammer and nail to make a pencil-sized eye-hole in the solid end of the can. Use sandpaper to rub off any sharp edges.

2. Using scissors, cut the ring edge off the second identical snap-on lid and keep the plastic disk.

3. Lay the 3 mirrors side by side on a flat surface, with the mirrored sides down. Tape these together so that they fold like a book along the seams.

4. If the mirrors are shorter than the cardboard tube, cut the tube down to the mirrors' length.

5. Fold the 3 mirrors into a pyramid shape, with the mirrored surface inside, and secure with tape.

6. Slide the mirror pyramid into the container and stuff a paper towel along the edge to hold it in place.

7. Lay the snap-on lid on the table so that the rim is up, making the lid look like a shallow saucer. Roll a small pea-sized ball of modeling clay and stick it in the center of this lid. The clay will act as a spacer to separate the snap-on lid from the plastic disk that will be placed on top.

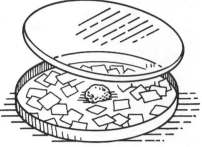

8. Sprinkle the bits of colored paper on the lid around the clay.

9. Top with the plastic disk, pressing it down lightly onto the clay.

10. Turn the cardboard tube—open end down—and press it onto the snap-on lid. Make sure the lid is on tight.

11. Aim the kaleidoscope's disk end at a sunny window or a lamp that's switched on. Look through the eyehole at the images on the mirrored surfaces.

12. Turn the cardboard tube or jiggle it to make the bits of paper move, changing the pattern you can see.

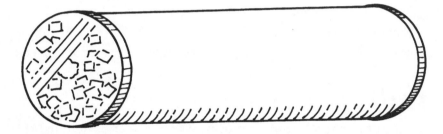

BRAIN BOOSTER

Light travels in a straight line and is reflected or bounced off a shiny surface, such as a mirror. In 1816, Sir David Brewster of Scotland discovered that when someone looked through a tube of mirrors, the light was bounced from one mirror to the other. Then the reflections created an interesting effect. He worked out the angles at which the mirrors needed to be set to make the reflected images appear to be in patterns. He named what he'd created a kaleidoscope, from the Greek words meaning "beautiful-form-to-see."

BONUS PACK

Go on a scavenger hunt to find things in nature that are transparent enough for light to shine through them. Use these objects and another set of snap-on lids to make an additional viewing disk for the kaleidoscope.

For More Science Toys Fun

Electricity (Make It Work! Science) by Wendy Baker, Alexandra Parsons, and Andrew Haslam (London: Two-Can Publishing LLC, 2000). This book is packed with science facts and imaginative investigations. Ages 9–12.

Gizmos and Gadgets: Creating Science Contraptions That Work (and Knowing Why) by Jill Franel Hauser (Charlotte, Vt.: Williamson Publishing, 1999). Directions for making fun stuff and explanations of the science basics that make these gadgets work. Ages 9–12.

Rubber-Band Banjos and a Java Jive Bass: Projects and Activities on the Science of Music and Sound by Alex Sabbeth (New York: John Wiley & Sons, 1997). A lively introduction to sound and musical instruments to build and play. Ages 9–12.

Science in Seconds with Toys: Over 100 Experiments You Can Do in Ten Minutes or Less by Jean Potter (New York: John Wiley & Sons, 1998). Easy-to-follow directions for toys made with household items. Explanations reveal the science that makes the toys fun. Ages 9–12.

Toy and Game Science by Peter Pentland and Pennie Stoyles (Broomall, Pa.: Chelsea House Publishers, 2002). This book is full of fun-filled science activities. Ages 9–12.

Wind Toys That Spin, Sing, Twirl and Whirl by Cindy Burda (New York: Sterling, 2000). Appealing designs for toys to make, while you investigate how wind powers them. Ages 8 and up.

Science Art

Create yummy chocolate sculptures. Find secret colors hidden in black ink. Learn how to make paint using Michelangelo's recipe. Float paint on water to create colorful greeting cards. And lots more! There's plenty of creative fun ahead, so jump into the action.

CHAPTER 16

Biology Art

Make Natural Glue ③

Conduct a stickiness test of three glues you can whip up yourself.

FUEL UP

flour glue (see the recipe in the box on this page)
gelatin glue (see the recipe in the box on page 204)
moo glue (see the recipe in the box on page 205)
plastic knife or craft stick
3 identical 4-inch (10-cm) squares of aluminum foil
3 identical 4-inch (10-cm) squares of cloth, such as from an old cotton T-shirt
3 identical 4-inch (10-cm) squares of white typing paper
poster board
pencil

BLAST OFF!

1. Prepare each of the glues.

2. Use the plastic knife to spread a thin layer of the flour glue on one square of each type of material. Press the squares—glue side down—onto the poster board. Label the samples to show which kind of glue is being tested.

3. Repeat step 2 with the gelatin glue and the moo glue.

Flour Glue

Pour 1 cup of white flour into a mixing bowl. Add 1 tablespoon of alum (available in grocery stores). Add about $\frac{1}{4}$ cup of water and stir to mix. Add another $\frac{1}{4}$ cup of water to the mixture and stir well.

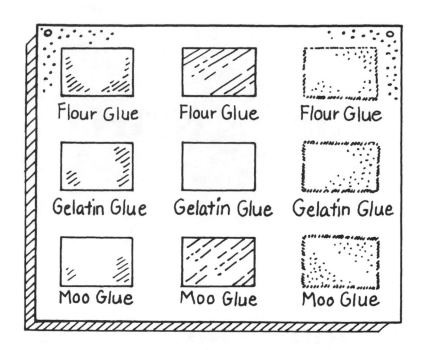

Gelatin Glue

Put ¼ cup of cool water into a heat-resistant mixing bowl. Sprinkle 1 envelope of unflavored gelatin onto the water and wait a few minutes to allow the gelatin granules to absorb water. Fill a quart-sized (0.9-l) saucepan half full of water. Have an adult bring the water to a boil on the stove and then shut off the heat.

Have an adult use oven mitts to set the mixing bowl on top of the saucepan of steaming hot water. Use the mixing spoon to stir until the gelatin is clear. As soon as the gelatin is clear, it is ready to use. If the gelatin becomes firm again, remove the mixing bowl and bring the water to a boil. Then return the bowl to the saucepan of steaming water.

4. Leave them overnight, then check the samples to decide which is the most effective glue. Check which glue samples are still stuck to the board. Which ones won't peel off easily?

Note: Unlike commercially produced glues, these glues do not contain preservatives, and they will mold.

BRAIN BOOSTER

Glue sticks by seeping into tiny openings in the two materials that you apply it to and then hardening. Or the molecules of the glue may get tangled up with the molecules of the materials that the glue is applied to, holding them together. There could even be a chemical reaction that fuses together the two materials the glue is between. How well the glue sticks is as much a result of the nature of the material that it's applied to, as it is due to the nature of the glue itself. That's why you probably found that none of these glues did a great job of sticking the aluminum foil. Flour

Moo Glue

Pour 1 pint (½ l) of skim milk and 6 tablespoons of vinegar into a nonmetallic saucepan, with a heatproof ceramic or enameled surface. Stir the mixture constantly over heat. As soon as the milk begins to form lumps, or curds, have an adult remove the pan from the heat. Let the pan sit until the lumps have settled. Have an adult pour the glue into a strainer or a colander to drain off the liquid. Pour the lumps into a mixing bowl. Then stir in ¼ cup of water and 1 tablespoon of baking soda. When the bubbling stops, the mixture will be glue.

glue, gelatin glue, and moo glue all do best when they can seep into tiny openings in the materials, like the ones in paper and cloth. Since the gelatin probably remained soft and sticky, it probably seemed to be the least effective.

Bonus Pack

Brainstorm other natural materials that might make good glues, such as egg white and plant sap. Check your ideas with an adult to be sure they are safe to try. Then repeat the test to check out how effective these glues are at making materials stick. Also, hold a family scavenger hunt around the house to search for things that are sticky. You'll find more, but don't miss these: tape, postage stamps, honey, decals, envelopes, and peanut butter.

That's Amazing

In 1970, Dr. Spencer Silver, a research chemist at 3M, thought that the new glue he was developing was a failure because it wasn't very effective at sticking surfaces together. Then Art Fry, a fellow worker at 3M, tried using some of this glue to make paper bookmarks that wouldn't fall out but also wouldn't damage the pages of his church hymnal. Presto! Post-It Notes were born. However, it took almost 10 years before the rest of the world caught on to the value of this only slightly sticky glue.

Make a Papier-Mâché Bird House ③

Put glue to work to create a strong multilayered material that gains strength from being stuck together. Then turn it into a waterproof birdhouse.

FUEL UP

newspaper
scissors
clean, empty half-gallon (2-l) plastic bottle
white glue
water
balloon
utility knife (for adult use only)
paintbrush
clear water-based enamel
toggle bolt
wire loop
acrylic craft paint
varnish
Note: This activity can be messy, so wear old clothes.

BLAST OFF!

1. Cover the work area with newspaper.

2. Get some more newspaper and cut 100 strips that are about 2 inches (5 cm) wide and 12 inches (30 cm) long. (You may need more, but this will be enough to start with.)

3. Have an adult cut the top off the plastic bottle.

4. Pour ½ cup of white glue and ½ cup of water into the bottom of the bottle and mix with your fingers.

5. Inflate the balloon. Tie a knot in the neck to seal it.

6. Dip the paper strips—one at time—into the glue. Wipe off the excess glue with your fingers, and smooth the strip onto the balloon.

7. Completely cover the balloon, including the knotted neck, with the paper strips

8. Let the glued paper dry completely. Then add another coat.

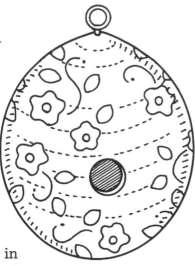

9. Repeat, covering the balloon with four layers of glued paper.

10. Once the paper is completely dry, have an adult use the utility knife to cut a round door in the side of the birdhouse. The circle should be 2 inches (5 cm) in diameter and placed about 4 inches (10 cm) above the fat end of the balloon. This will also pop the balloon that's inside. *Note: To make the house suitable for a specific kind of bird living in your area, check with a local nature center or a veterinarian about what size of a hole to cut for a door.*

11. Working outdoors, coat the inside of the birdhouse with water-based enamel.

12. Have an adult use the scissors point to poke 3 drainage holes in the bottom of the birdhouse. If you live where the weather gets very warm, also have the adult poke 6 ventilation holes about midway down the side and encircling the birdhouse.

13. Have an adult attach the toggle bolt to the pointed end of the birdhouse. Twist on a wire loop that you can use to hang up the birdhouse.

14. Paint the outside of the birdhouse with the acrylic paint. You can make it all one color or paint a design, such as flowers and leaves.

15. When the paint is dry, top with a coat of varnish.

16. Hang your birdhouse from a tree branch and see which birds make it their home.

BRAIN BOOSTER

In the second century, the Chinese invented papier-mâché as a way to recycle paper. Because it is made up of many layers of paper bonded together by glue, the papier-mâché was also much stronger than just a sheet of paper. In fact, it was so much stronger that the Chinese used it to make helmets for their soldiers. Papier-mâché also became a popular way to shape paper to create masks, jewelry boxes, bowls, and more. In the 1800s, papier-mâché was used to build a boat and even some houses.

BONUS PACK

Use papier-mâché to create a bracelet. Start with a cardboard ring that fits around your wrist with plenty of room to spare. Next, wrap this with layers of papier-mâché. When it's dry, paint on a design, and when the paint is dry, cover with craft varnish.

THAT'S AMAZING

In 1807, manufacturers started to produce dolls commercially by pressing papier-mâché over molds that formed the doll's head. The face was then painted on. Sometimes glass eyes were set into the papier-mâché head.

Save Leaf Skeletons ②

Take a close look at a leaf to see and feel the raised network of veins. Go on a walk to collect several different kinds of leaves for this project.

Fuel Up

3-quart (2.8-l) saucepan

water

at least 3 leaves with interesting vein patterns

tongs

newspaper

old toothbrush (Make sure you have an adult's permission to use this.)

gold paint (optional)

safety goggles (If you're painting, use them to keep splattering paint from getting into your eyes.)

white glue

waxed paper

black or another dark color of construction paper

cardboard (optional)

Blast Off!

1. Fill the pan two-thirds full of water and bring to a boil.

2. Turn down the heat and have an adult drop the leaves into the water. Use the tongs to submerge the leaves.

3. Simmer for about an hour.

4. Turn off the heat and let the water cool.

5. Remove the leaves from the water and spread them out flat on the newspaper.

6. Use the toothbrush to gently remove the leaf tissue from between the veins, leaving the leaf's skeleton. Don't worry if a few small veins break.

7. If you'd like to paint the leaf skeleton, do it now and let it dry. Wear safety goggles.

8. Make a small puddle of white glue on waxed paper.

9. Move the leaf skeleton through the glue and place it on a sheet of dark paper. Glue each leaf skeleton to a separate sheet of paper or group several on one sheet. You may also want to look up the leaves in a plant or tree identification book and label the leaf skeletons.

10. You may want to finish by gluing the construction paper on cardboard.

Brain Booster

A leaf's veins carry water and minerals to the leaf's cells. They carry the food produced in the leaf's cells away to be stored in the roots, the stems, and the seeds. They also form the skeleton (the supporting framework of the leaf). Removing the leaf's fleshy tissue reveals how strong this skeleton is and how thoroughly it branches to reach every part of the leaf. It's also possible to see the different skeletal patterns that are characteristic of different kinds of plant leaves.

Bonus Pack

Play a game using any leaves that you didn't turn into skeletons or you could collect more. Sort the leaves into two groups: those that have toothed edges and those that don't. Now, think of at least five other traits that you could use to sort the leaves. You'll think of others, but here are a few to get you started: oval leaves, big leaves, hand-shaped leaves.

Rub-a-Tree Place Mat ③

Many kinds of trees can be identified by their unique bark, the armorlike covering of the tree. Turn what you learn from a tree investigation into keepsake place mats.

Fuel Up

4-inch (10-cm) squares of white construction paper (one for each tree that you'll do a rubbing of)
crayons
tree identification book showing trees that are common to your location
pencil
colored poster board
scissors
colored construction paper
black permanent marking pen
sheet of white paper
white glue
clear plastic contact paper

BLAST OFF!

1. Go on a family bark-collecting walk. Whenever you discover a tree with interesting-looking bark, collect a rubbing. Do that by pressing a square of paper against the tree and rubbing across the paper with the crayon. Making broad strokes with an exposed side of the crayon works best.

2. Use the tree identification book to find the name of the tree. Record this in pencil on the back of the bark rubbing.

3. Back home, cut out a piece of poster board the size you'd like to use for a place mat.

4. Using scissors, cut out 2-by-4-inch (5-by-10 cm) ribbons of colored construction paper—one for each bark rubbing. Use the black marking pen to print the name of each tree on a separate paper ribbon. Trim as needed, so that the strip is just the size of the name.

5. Use the marking pen to write a number somewhere on the front of each bark rubbing.

6. Arrange several tree rubbings on the poster board.

7. On a separate sheet of paper, make a master list showing the numbers of the rubbings you selected for that place mat, and next to each, glue on the ribbon showing the name of that tree.

8. Glue the rubbings on the poster board, turning some and making some overlap. Be sure the number is always visible.

9. Decorate the areas around the rubbings with crayon drawings of trees or tree leaves.

10. Glue the master list on the back of the poster board.

11. Label both the front and the back of the poster board with the challenge "Can you name that tree?"

12. To turn the poster board into a washable place mat, cover it with clear contact paper.

13. Make enough additional place mats with other bark rubbings for each family member to have one.

BRAIN BOOSTER

The bark is the outer coating on a tree. It is actually made up of two layers—the dead protective coat you see and the living inner layer, called the cork. As the tree's trunk grows and expands, the bark cracks and splits. It's possible to identify many trees by their characteristic bark. Black walnut bark is nearly black and has deep furrows between strong ridges. Pine tree bark consists of rough, scaly plates. Honey locust bark is studded with large, branched thorns. Many kinds of eucalyptus trees have peeling bark that hangs from the tree like a tattered coat. Whatever it looks like, bark protects the tree from harsh weather conditions, disease, insects, and sometimes even fire.

Bonus Pack

Make bark rubbings on 4-inch (10-cm) cloth squares, using textile markers. Also use a textile marker to label each square with the tree's name. Sew enough squares together to cover a large bath towel. Sew along the edges to make the towel the back of the quilt.

That's Amazing

In Fiji, Samoa, Tonga, and other Polynesian Islands, the bark of the paper mulberry tree is used to make a kind of cloth, called tapa cloth. The bark is stripped off the tree and pounded flat. Then the bark strips are glued together. In North America, the early woodland tribes of Indians covered their houses with birch bark. They also used birch bark to cover the wooden frames of their canoes. The seams where the sheets of bark overlapped were sealed with pitch, a sticky dark material obtained from some evergreen trees.

Spray a Leaf Shirt ③

Go on a walk to discover some of the most interesting shapes in nature—broad, flat tree leaves. Then follow these easy steps to capture those shapes and wear them.

Fuel Up

leaves
plastic grocery bag
newspaper
rocks
hand pump spray bottle
1 color of textile paint
scissors
cardboard
white cotton T-shirt

Blast Off!

1. Collect leaves from broadleaf trees and put them into the grocery bag.

2. Back home, immediately spread the leaves flat between layers of newspaper. Top with rocks to flatten them even more.

3. Fill the spray bottle with textile paint.

4. Using scissors, cut the cardboard to fit inside the T-shirt.

5. Working outdoors, cover a work area with newspaper. Lay the T-shirt on the newspapers, front side up.

6. Arrange leaves on the front of the T-shirt.

7. Spray on the textile paint until the leaves and the area around them are covered. Be careful not to spray the paint on so heavily that it forms globs.

8. Have an adult wearing rubber gloves carefully lift off the leaves.

9. Let the paint completely dry.

Brain Booster

Your T-shirt will have interesting white leaf shapes on a colored background. Have you ever wondered why tree leaves have the shapes they do? It's to help every leaf on the tree get as much sunlight exposure as possible. A tree's leaves are its food source. Through a process called photosynthesis, green chlorophyll molecules in the leaves absorb light energy from the sun and use it to change carbon dioxide gas and water into sugar and a waste gas, oxygen. Because it's so important that the leaves be exposed to sunlight, leaves have lobes and indentations to prevent them from shading the other leaves on the tree. Some are even made up of many small leaflets to let light slip through to the lower branches as they flutter in the wind. The leaves on a tree are also arranged in one of two ways: in a single layer or in a multilayer. In a single-layer arrangement, the branches are arranged like umbrella spokes, so that the leaves form a canopy that's exposed to the sun. In a multilayer arrangement, leaves on

upper branches may be smaller than those on lower branches, to let the sunlight filter down. Notice how the leaves you collect are arranged to help the tree's food factories get all the sunlight they need. Use a tree identification book to find out what kind of trees your leaves came from.

Bonus Pack

Take a new view of a tree's leaves by spreading a blanket on the ground and looking up through the branches. A well-known painter, Georgia O'Keeffe, once painted this view of a tree. If possible, take a look at her painting called *The Lawrence Tree*, online or in a book. Encourage budding artists to paint a tree's portrait using this same point of view.

Save a Scent

Create a potpourri, a scented collection of material, to enhance your home environment or to give as a gift.

Fuel Up

 a collection of good-smelling bits from nature, such as lavender flowers or leaves, orange peel, marigold blooms, rose petals, cinnamon bark, geranium leaves, and small pinecones
 newspaper
 6-inch (15-cm) square of cotton cloth
 ribbon

Blast Off!

1. Spread piles of the different kinds of scent materials on newspaper and leave them until completely dry.

2. Combine materials to create a scent symphony—a mixture of scents that are even better together than alone.

3. Scoop a handful of the potpourri, the scented material you mixed together, onto the center of a cloth square.

4. Pull together all of the edges of the fabric to cover the potpourri. Tie with ribbon to keep the fabric edges closed over the potpourri, forming a sachet.

5. Trim off any excess ribbon.

Brain Booster

Diffusion is the reason that a sachet of potpourri can scent an entire drawer or even a room. To see how diffusion works, drip one drop of food coloring into a glass full of water and watch it slowly spread until all of the water is tinted. Diffusion is the process of something spreading from where there is a lot to where there is only a little. This is what happens as tiny scent molecules spread through the air. A potpourri's scent will fade over time. When it does, untie the packet, throw out the old scent material, and refresh the sachet with new potpourri.

Bonus Pack

Make a pomander ball, a special way to preserve the lovely scent of lemons or oranges. First, wash and dry the fruit. Use push pins to tack two pieces of ribbon or lace around a lemon or an orange, dividing it into four parts. Use a nail to make rows of holes in each section of the fruit. Stick a whole clove into each hole. Repeat until the fruit is covered with rows of cloves. Next, on waxed paper, mix together ¼ cup of ground cinnamon and 1 tablespoon of powdered orris root (a natural preservative available from health food stores and craft stores). Roll the fruit in this mixture, then place it on paper towels in a cool, dark location. Leave it for 3 or 4 weeks until the fruit has completely dried out. In Colonial times, pomander balls were used as Christmas decorations, adding a special spicy scent to the holidays. Women also carried small ones in their handkerchiefs to sniff if the street odors were unpleasant.

Create a One-of-a-Kind Fingerprint Frame ③

Start by using a magnifying glass to take a close look at the pattern of ridges on the tip of each finger. Then let those ridged fingertips get creative.

Fuel Up

photo frame
scissors
white or light-colored construction paper

family photo: select one small enough—or choose a large-enough frame—to allow
about a 2-inch (5-cm) border between the photo and the frame)

pencil

ink pad

transparent tape

Blast Off!

1. Take out the cardboard backing in the photo frame and, using scissors, cut the construction paper to this size.

2. Place the family photo in the center of this paper and lightly trace around it with a pencil. Then set the photo aside.

3. Plan the pattern that you'll arrange the fingerprints in. For example, they could become flowers with a center print surrounded by "petal" prints. Be sure that the pattern includes prints from every family member in the photo.

4. Make prints on the construction paper around the outline of the photo by pressing an index finger onto the inkpad, then pressing the inked fingertip onto the construction paper.

5. Repeat until you have completed your planned fingerprint pattern and let the prints dry.

6. Put loops of tape on the back of the photo at the corners. Then press the photo onto the paper so that it fits inside the outlined box, where it is now surrounded by a unique fingerprint border.

7. Put the photo and the border into the frame.

Brain Booster

The ridges on people's fingertips are like treads on tires. They help provide friction, making it possible to grip things and hang on. The pattern of each person's fingerprints is completely unique. Even the pattern on each finger is slightly different from any of the others. However, people do tend to have fingerprints that fit into one of three general categories: loop, arch, or whorl.

Loop　　Arch　　Whorl

BONUS PACK

If you haven't already tried it, check out "Use Your Fingertip to Make a Glass Ring" (see page 115). Also test how changing the amount of water in the goblet affects the tone that's produced.

Capture a Shadow Portrait ③

Discover that shadows occur everywhere that there's light and they give things shape and texture. Before cameras, shadows were also an inexpensive way to capture a loved one's image.

FUEL UP

masking tape
white butcher paper or sheet of poster board
bright light, such as a 6-volt lantern flashlight
pencil
scissors
black construction paper or poster board
white mat board
white glue

BLAST OFF!

1. Tape the white paper to the wall at head height.

2. Have the person whose shadow portrait you want to make stand sideways next to the paper.

3. Have a helper hold the light so that it casts a shadow of the person's silhouette on the paper.

4. Use the pencil to outline the silhouette of the person's head.

5. Cut out the white paper shadow shape.

6. Place the shadow shape on the black paper and trace around it.

7. Cut out the black paper shadow shape.

8. Place on the mat board and glue in place.

Brain Booster

Light travels in a straight line. A shadow is an area where the light is blocked. Light creates two kinds of shadows: form shadows and cast shadows. Form shadows are the ones that appear on an object, an animal, a plant, or a person. They let us see wrinkles and bumps, for example. Without these shadows, everything would look flat. That would make the world dull. It would also make it difficult for us to navigate the world. For example, imagine trying to walk up stairs where there are no shadows to define the steps. Cast shadows are the shadows of a whole object, an animal, a plant, or a person. Outdoors, cast shadows are longer when the sun is low in the sky during the early morning and the late afternoon, and they are shorter around noon.

Bonus Pack

Go outdoors on a shadow hunt and take along a measuring tape. Search for the following shadows: the longest, the shortest, the fattest, and the skinniest.

Make a Book to Trick Your Eyes ②

Create an animated mini-flick to explore how you see. Before you start, look out a window at a bright sunny scene or at a brightly lit room, then quickly shut your eyes. The brief afterimage of the scene you see is a glimpse of the phenomenon that makes animation work.

Fuel Up

6 sheets white typing paper
scissors
pencil
crayons
stapler

Blast Off!

1. Fold each sheet of paper into fourths.

2. Using scissors, cut the sections apart, creating 24 pages.

3. Draw a tree with bare branches in the center of one page.

4. Put a second page on top of the first. Hold the two pages up to a window and trace the tree onto the second page. Repeat this process so that you have 24 identical pages.

5. Now, using crayons, add leaves to the trees. On pages 1 and 2, show green leaves all over the branches. On pages 3 through 9, show increasingly more of the leaves in red and yellow. On pages 10 through 23, show fewer and fewer leaves on the tree and more piled up on the ground. On page 24, show the tree bare.

6. Stack the pages in order from the fully leafed green tree through the bare tree.

7. Staple the pages together along the left-hand side near the top, the middle, and the bottom to create a book.

8. Watch while flipping rapidly through the pages from front to back.

Brain Booster

You are able to see when light reflected from an object enters your eye and strikes light-sensitive cells on the retina at the back of your eye, then these cells send signals to your brain. As soon as your brain analyzes the signals, you become aware of the image. Your brain does its job in a flash, but in the meantime, the light-sensitive cells retain an image for about one-fifth of a second after it's no longer visible. This is called "persistence of vision." It means that if another image appears within the time the first image is retained, the two are interpreted as running together. It also helps that the brain mentally bridges the two images together.

Animated films—in fact, all movies—are really a series of still images displayed one after the other so rapidly that your brain interprets them as moving. Early movies were called "flicks" because the images weren't displayed quickly enough, and they appeared to flicker. Today, images for movies are displayed at 24 frames per second—this is fast enough to give the illusion of action without the flicker.

BONUS PACK

Zoopraxiscope is the name given to the earliest kind of movie projector— a device that spins around to let you view images in sequence. To make your own, cut a strip of paper that can be wrapped around a round carton, such as an oatmeal carton. Divide this strip into equal sections. Then draw a sequence of images on the sections, such as pictures showing a dropped ball falling to the ground and then bouncing up again. Next, have an adult poke a hole in the bottom of the carton big enough for a pencil to fit snugly. Glue the image strip around the carton. Then, holding the pencil, spin the carton around and watch the image strip.

String a Seed Necklace ③

Investigate the diversity of seeds, while you create this wearable art. Collect wild seeds on a nature walk, select seeds from the garden, or go on a seed hunt at the grocery store. Select large seeds that have an interesting shape and color.

FUEL UP

mixing bowl

hot water

at least 5 kinds of large seeds, such as sunflower, kidney beans, squash, or pumpkin (about 20 of each kind of seed)

embroidery needle

24-inch (60-cm) piece of dental floss

paper towels

BLAST OFF!

1. Fill the mixing bowl half full of hot tap water.

2. Place the seeds in the water and let them soak for about 15 minutes or until soft enough to poke the needle through.

3. Thread the needle with dental floss.

4. Arrange some of each kind of seed on the paper towel to create a pattern.

5. Scoop a small handful of seeds out onto the paper towel.

6. Thread the seeds on the line, following the pattern you created. Repeat the pattern until the line is filled to within 4 inches (10 cm) of the end.

7. Slide the seeds toward the middle of the line so that there is free string at either end. Tie the ends of the line together.

8. Let the necklace dry overnight before wearing it.

Brain Booster

Seeds are baby plants, called embryos, with a package of stored food inside a protective seed coat. To see the plant embryo, soak six bean seeds overnight. Then carefully pry one seed open, revealing the plant embryo and the two masses of stored starch that will help the little plant start to grow. To see a seed sprout, soak a paper towel in water, squeeze out the excess, fold the towel into fourths, and place it inside a sandwich-sized, self-sealing plastic bag. Place the remaining seeds on the wet towel, seal all but one corner of the bag, and lay the bag in a warm place. Be sure the bag is turned so the seeds are on top of the towel. Sprouts will appear in a few days. To see the plants continue to grow, transfer the sprouts to small pots full of potting soil.

Bonus Pack

Use seeds to create a mosaic, a picture made up of different pieces put together. Draw a picture on sturdy cardboard, such as a panel from a box. Keep the picture simple, such as a flower with a center circle surrounded by oval petals. Collect different kinds of seeds with interesting colors, shapes, and textures. Use these seeds to "paint" each part of the picture, including the background. Plan which seeds to use on each picture part. Next, spread white glue on one part of the picture. Lay seeds, one by one, on this area until it is covered. Then continue to spread glue and add seeds until the entire picture is covered. For kitchen art, make a mosaic entirely from spice seeds, such as cloves, peppercorns, fennel seeds, coriander seeds, sesame seeds, and others.

CHAPTER 17

Chemistry Art

Make Weathered Stamps ③

As you create stamp blocks, explore how weathering carves away rocks. Then use the stamps to transform paper bags into gift bags.

FUEL UP

pencil

4 2-inch (5-cm) square blocks of Styrofoam

sandpaper

pebble

at least 2 inked stamp pads with different colors (or spread acrylic paint on a clean sponge)

brown paper bags

BLAST OFF!

1. Draw a simple design, such as a heart, a fish, or a triangle, on one side of one of the Styrofoam blocks.

2. Use the sandpaper to rub away the Styrofoam around the outside of the shape. Rub away enough that the shape stands out from the rest of the surface.

3. Press down on the shape with the pebble to add dents.

4. Repeat this process to make three other stamp blocks.

5. Press the stamps on the stamp pad or the paint-covered sponge.

6. Press the stamp on the paper bag. Repeat to create a pattern with the different stamp shapes.

BRAIN BOOSTER

Weathering is the natural process that breaks down and wears away the surfaces of rocks. Nature's sandpaper is wind and water. Wind blasts sand particles at the rocks. Fast-moving streams carry along rocks, bumping them into other rocks on the bottom and the sides of the stream.

THAT'S AMAZING

Balanced Rock in Idaho's Salmon Falls Creek Canyon is an unusual wind-weathered rock. This giant rock—nearly 48 feet (15 m) tall—is balanced on a rock pedestal that's only 3 feet (0.9 m) tall and 17 inches (42 cm) wide. How long this rock stays balanced will depend on how fast the wind erodes its pedestal.

BONUS PACK

Use textile paint to stamp a design on a plain book bag.

Create Paint Like the Masters ②

Investigate how pigments (coloring matter) can be suspended in a binding material, while you make paint the way famous painters like Michelangelo, Van Gogh, and Cezanne did.

FUEL UP

Before you start, go on a family scavenger hunt to collect soil that is at least two different shades, such as reddish-brown and very black-brown.

    rock
    old dinner plate (Be sure you have an adult's permission to use it.)
    linseed oil (available at art supply stores)
    craft sticks
    mineral spirits (available at art supply stores)
    pencil
    small prepared oil painting canvas (available at art supply stores)

Blast Off!

1. If the soil is damp, let it dry out completely before starting. Then, working outdoors, use the rock to hammer one color of soil until it's a fine powder.

2. Put 1 teaspoon of the powdered soil on the plate.

3. Add linseed oil a few drops at a time, mixing with a craft stick until the mixture becomes a paste.

4. If the paste is lumpy, add a couple of drops of mineral spirits.

5. Add more linseed oil to the paste until it is the thickness of creamy butter.

6. Sketch a picture or a design on the canvas with a pencil.

7. Paint one section with the paint you made.

8. Repeat the steps to create other earth-colored paints.

9. Finish painting the picture in earth tones.

Brain Booster

People have been creating pictures with colored paint since ancient times. However, until recently, artists had to create their own paint. In fact, recipes for certain colors were once carefully guarded secrets. Paint is made up of two things: pigment and binder. Pigment is colored material that won't dissolve. Binder is a material in which the pigment can be suspended and made to stick to a surface like canvas. The first pigments were ground-up materials that occurred in nature, including earth, rocks, eggshells, and tree bark. One shade of yellow was obtained by using cow urine. Later, chemists created man-made pigments. The first artificially produced paint was Prussian blue, produced from iron in 1724.

Bonus Pack

Use the following recipe to whip up different colors of soapy finger paints. Then paint outdoors on a warm, sunny day and clean up with a hose. Or let youngsters paint in the tub and finish up with a bath. Paint recipe: For each color, use a fork to beat together ½ cup of soap flakes (not detergent), food coloring, and enough water to make a paste.

Paint with the Secret Colors in Black Ink ②

Investigate how materials settle out of liquids, as you create a picture that transforms itself almost by magic. Before you start, pour the following into a clear pint-sized (0.5-l) jar with a screw-on lid: ¼ cup of sand, 2 tablespoons of pebbles, 1 ping-pong-ball-sized rock. Fill the container two-thirds full of water, screw on the lid, and shake. Allow time for the ingredients to settle and take a close look at the layering. The larger, heavier stones are on the bottom and the smaller, lighter ones are on top. Now, find out that the same thing happens with coloring matter.

FUEL UP

black water color marking pen
white construction paper
2 full 2-liter plastic soft drink bottles
cake pan
string
masking tape
books
water

BLAST OFF!

1. Use the black marking pen to create a picture on the white paper.
2. Set one soft drink bottle on either side of the cake pan.
3. Tie a piece of string between the necks of the two bottles.
4. Tape the paper to the string. The bottom edge of the paper should just touch the bottom of the cake pan. Elevate the bottles on books, if necessary, to raise the paper.
5. Pour in just enough water to cover the bottom of the cake pan.

6. Watch as the water moves up the paper through the areas colored with the black marking pen.

BRAIN BOOSTER

The water traveled up the paper through a process called capillary action. Once the water reached the black ink, it dissolved some of this and carried it along, too. This is when the transformation started. Inks and paints appear to be different colors because they absorb certain wavelengths of the light that strikes them and they reflect others. Red ink or paint looks red because it reflects only red light and absorbs all of the other wavelengths. A combination of all the colors—red, blue, green, and yellow—absorbs so much light that this combination appears black. After the water dissolves the black ink from the marking pen, the individual colors separate. Some of these pigments are a little heavier than others. They soon settle out and become visible. The lighter ones are carried along farther before they settle out. So the black picture develops a rainbow effect as capillary action carries the water along.

Note: Add more water to the pan, as needed, to keep the capillary action going. To stop the water from climbing higher at any point, simply remove the paper from the water.

BONUS PACK

If you haven't already enjoyed the activity "Create a Juicy T-Shirt" (see page 8), try it now to see more capillary action.

Transfer a Picture ②

Make inks dissolve and then relocate them to transfer a picture.

FUEL UP

2 tablespoons soap powder, such as scrapings from a bar of hand soap (not laundry detergent)

¼ cup hot water

pint-sized (0.5-l) jar with a screw-on lid

metal spoon

1 tablespoon turpentine

paper towels

old sheet or plastic trash bags

cardboard to fit inside shirt

clean white T-shirt

safety pin (optional)

clean paintbrush

color picture from a recent newspaper or one recently printed on a color printer— choose a picture without text

BLAST OFF!

1. Pour the soap powder and hot water into the jar.
2. Stir until dissolved.
3. Add the turpentine, stir again, and let the solution cool. This is your transfer solution.
4. Dry off the spoon with a paper towel.
5. Cover the work area with the old sheet or plastic bags.
6. Put the cardboard inside the T-shirt. Place the shirt—front side up—on the work area and smooth the material flat. You may want to pin the shirt in the back to make it stay flat and unwrinkled in the front.
7. Use the brush to paint the transfer solution all over the picture.
8. Count to 50 (or wait about 10 to 20 seconds) to allow the solution to soak in.
9. Place the picture—solution side down—on the front of the T-shirt.
10. Pressing down, rub the back of the spoon firmly all over the picture.
11. Peel off the picture and throw it away.
12. Rinse the brush and put the cap on the jar to store the solution.

BRAIN BOOSTER

Something dissolves when it breaks down and moves into a solution. Many kinds of materials, including sugar and salt, dissolve in water. Some paints, like tempera paint powder, dissolve in water, too. Other paints and inks will not dissolve in water, but they will dissolve in alcohol and turpentine, which is a semifluid resin that comes from trees—mainly pine trees. In this activity, the soap in the transfer solution helped to break down any oils that coated the paper. Then the turpentine dissolved some of the pigment, or coloring matter, that was used to print the picture. Rubbing pushed the dissolved pigment into the cloth fibers. The result was a copy of the original image. However, since the image was turned over, the copy was in reverse. This means that any text would have been reversed, too.

BONUS PACK

Use this image transfer method to make a theme quilt. Print one image on each quilt square, then sew the squares together. Sew a backing cloth to the assembled sheet of squares. If you have access to digital images on a computer, make color prints of family photos to create a quilt of family memories.

Print with Water ③

Use the fact that oil and water don't mix to create marbleized paper the way it's been done since the 1600s.

Fuel Up

scissors

white typing paper

newspapers

aluminum pie pan

bottled water (tap water can contain chemicals that affect the results)

red, blue, and yellow oil-base enamel paints (small bottles are available at craft and hobby stores)

toothpick

Note: This can be messy, so wear old clothes or wear a plastic trash bag with holes cut out for your head and arms.

Blast Off!

1. Using scissors, cut the paper into fourths.

2. Cover the work area with newspapers.

3. Fill the pan about two-thirds full of water.

4. When the water in the pan is still, drip a little of each color of paint onto the surface.

5. Draw a toothpick through the paint to create a pattern.

6. Place a piece of paper on the paint. Press lightly to make sure the entire surface of the paper has made contact.

7. Lift the paper off the water and lay it—paint side up—on the newspaper.

8. Let the printed paper dry.

Brain Booster

Oil-based paints float on water because they are less dense, or thick, than water. Marbleized paper was developed in the 1600s and was used to decorate the endpapers and even the edges of books. The name comes from the fact that the colored patterns in the paper looked like the natural patterns in marble, a type of rock. Marbleized paper was so highly valued that the process for producing it was kept as a family secret by the craftsmen who made it. Masters of this printing process created special patterns, such as a feather pattern, using combs and rakes. The secret was so well guarded that it didn't slip out until the middle of the nineteenth century.

Bonus Pack

Brainstorm some ways to use this special paper. Here are a few to get you started: (1) use the printed papers to create greeting cards; (2) glue a strip on the top of a sheet of plain paper to decorate stationery; and (3) glue two sheets around an empty soup can to transform it into a pencil holder.

Sculpt Shapes You Can Eat ③

The **melting point** is the temperature at which a solid turns into a liquid. By having this chocolate mixture at just the right temperature, you can create a material that's perfect for shaping—and munching.

Fuel Up

10 ounces (283.5 g) chocolate chips
microwave-safe container
microwave (or saucepan over a large pan of hot water)
mixing spoon
⅓ cup light corn syrup
waxed paper

Blast Off!

1. Put the chocolate in a microwave-safe dish and heat in the microwave—about 1 minute or until melted. Or have an adult melt the chocolate in the saucepan by holding it so that the bottom is in contact with boiling water.

2. Stir in the corn syrup until well blended.

3. Pour the mixture onto waxed paper.

4. Wash and dry your hands.

5. After 2 minutes, use your hands to spread the chocolate into a flat sheet.

6. Cover with more waxed paper and leave until stiff—about 2 hours or overnight.

7. With clean hands, shape the stiff but pliable chocolate into shapes.

8. Chill until firm.

9. Show off the sculpture. Then let everyone enjoy munching this work of art.

BRAIN BOOSTER

Chocolate has a low melting point; it will melt at your body temperature—98°F (36°C). Find out for yourself by holding a couple of chocolate chips on your palm. They will soon become soft. In this mixture, the corn syrup helped to thicken the mixture. It also raised the melting point of the chocolate just enough to make it flexible, not gooey.

BONUS PACK

What happens if something is made of two kinds of matter with different melting points? Find out for yourself. Be sure your hands are clean and dry. Then hold two M&M candies on your palm and cover them with your other hand. Don't squeeze. Wait 2 minutes. Then place the candies on a clean paper towel and break them in half with a fork or spoon. The chocolate inside will be melted, while the candy shell will still be solid.

THAT'S AMAZING

Using a secret recipe, Hershey's produces a chocolate bar called the "desert bar." This was developed especially for armies during warfare in desert countries. It stays solid even when the temperature soars to 140°F (60°C).

Ukrainian Eggs  ②

These simple but elegant decorated eggs have patterns that are created by using wax to block colored dyes from touching certain parts of the shell.

FUEL UP

pencil
at least 3 empty eggshells (see How to Empty Eggshells on page 231)

plastic cups
red, yellow, and blue food coloring
hot water
vinegar
spoon
paper towel
white or yellow crayon
paper plate
microwave
black permanent marking pen (fine point)

Blast Off!

1. Use a pencil to draw a simple design of lines and shapes on the eggshells.

2. For each color dye, mix these ingredients together in a paper cup: ¼ teaspoon of food coloring, ¾ cup of hot water, and 1 tablespoon of white vinegar. The vinegar helps to set the color.

3. Put the eggs—one at a time—in the yellow dye. Leave for about 1 minute or up to 5 minutes for a darker hue.

4. Use the spoon to move the eggs to a paper towel.

5. Once the eggs are dry, use the white or yellow crayon to color over any part that you want to remain yellow.

6. Put the eggs—one at a time—into the red dye. Leave for 1 to 5 minutes. Then use the spoon to move them to the paper towel.

7. Use the crayon to color over any part that is to remain orange.

8. Put the eggs—one at a time—into the blue dye. Leave for 1 to 5 minutes. Then use the spoon to move them to the paper towel.

9. Set the dried eggshells on the paper plate and put the plate in the microwave.

10. Microwave for 7 to 10 seconds or until the wax can be wiped off easily with a paper towel.

11. Use the fine-tip marking pen to outline the colored areas or to draw a design over the existing colors.

How to Empty Eggshells

To empty an egg without cracking the shell, use a pin to poke a small hole in each end of the egg. Enlarge the hole at the bigger end of the egg. Poke a toothpick into that hole and wiggle it to break the yolk. Hold the egg over a bowl, with the big end down. Blow into the smaller hole in short puffs to force the contents out the bigger hole. Rinse the eggshell and set it on a paper towel to dry.

BRAIN BOOSTER

The eggshell became colored when the dye penetrated the shell material. The crayon is made of wax, and the wax didn't penetrate the shell. Instead, it coated the shell and prevented any coloring matter from reaching the shell. Heat caused the wax to melt so that it could easily be wiped away.

BONUS PACK

Use the contents of the blown eggs to make scrambled eggs. Put the eggs between two slices of toast and add a slice of cheese for a scrambled egg sandwich treat.

CHAPTER 18

Physics Art

Make a Mobile ②

Learn how to balance weights to create suspended art that comes to life when there's a breeze.

FUEL UP

scissors
3 sturdy paper plates
hole punch
colored markers
silver and gold glitter
ruler
dental floss
embroidery needle
2 plastic straws
white glue
coat hanger
transparent tape
6-inch (15-cm) piece of sturdy string
pliers (adult use only)

BLAST OFF!

1. Using scissors, cut 5 identical fish, about the size of large eggs, from the centers of the paper plates.

2. Use the hole punch to make a hole in the dorsal fin or the middle of the upper back of each fish.

3. Decorate the fish using the colored markers and glitter.

4. Cut two 24-inch (60-cm) pieces of floss. Thread one piece through the needle and then through one straw, so that part of the floss hangs out either end of the straw.

5. Tie each end of the floss to a fish through the hole in its back.

6. Thread the second piece of floss through the other straw and tie the ends to two more fish.

7. Gently tug one end of the floss, so that the fish tied to it hangs down below the fish at the other end of the straw.

8. Cut a 10-inch (25-cm) piece of floss. Tie it to the middle of one of the straws and anchor with a dab of glue.

9. Cut a 15-inch (37-cm) piece of floss. Tie it to the middle of the other straw and anchor with a dab of glue.

10. Tie the straw with the shorter piece of floss to one corner of the bottom of the hanger. Anchor with tape.

11. Tie the straw with the longer piece of floss to the opposite bottom corner of the hanger. Anchor with tape.

12. Cut a 6-inch (15-cm) piece of floss. Tie one end to the fifth fish through the hole in its back. Tie the free end of the floss to the middle of the bottom of the hanger. Anchor with tape.

13. Tie the two ends of the string together to form a loop. Slip this over the hanger's hook.

14. Have an adult use pliers to squeeze the hanger's hook so that the string loop won't slip off.

15. Hang the hanger mobile where it can turn in the wind.

16. The two straws should hang straight. If not, slide the thread slightly, as needed, until the straw is balanced and hanging straight. Add a dab of glue at either end of the straw to secure the floss in this position.

BRAIN BOOSTER

Every object has a balancing point—the point at which its weight is evenly distributed. This may not be in the center of the object. For example, try to balance a wooden baseball bat on just two fingers. The bat is heavier at one end than at the other, so its balancing point is closer to the heavier end. Try balancing other objects on one or two fingers to find their balancing points. In the 1930s, Alexander Calder developed the idea of creating a moving sculpture by suspending objects from their balancing points. These sculptures were named mobiles because air currents were enough to set them in motion. One of Calder's most famous works is called *Circus*. It uses cork, wood, cloth, and wire shapes to represent circus performers in action.

Bonus Pack

Try to create a mobile made of objects with a theme, such as seasonal decorations or things that are commonly found on a desk. Remember, the key to success is to balance pairs of objects.

Create a Wind Chime ③

Listen to the wind with this instrument that you can make from things around the house.

Fuel Up

scissors
2-liter colored-plastic soft drink bottle with a screw-on plastic cap
hole punch
ruler
string
7 metal items, such as old silverware, old keys, metal washers, bolts,
   or any combination of metal items
duct tape

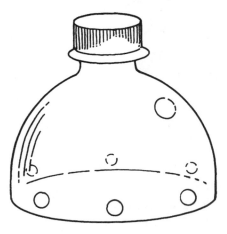

Blast Off!

1. Have an adult cut the top off the bottle about 2 inches (5 cm) below the curved neck. Use the hole punch to make six equally spaced holes around the lower edge of the bottle top. Screw off the bottle cap.

2. Cut six 12-inch (30-cm) pieces of string.

3. Thread one end of each string through a hole in the bottle top and tie a knot.

4. Tie the other end of each string around one of your metal objects. Don't worry if the strings are different lengths. You may want to anchor the strings to the bottle top and each object with duct tape.

5. Cut an approximately 1-yard (1-m) piece of string. Make a loop in one end of the string and tie a knot.

6. About 3 inches (8 cm) down from the looped end, tie a second knot.

7. Poke a hole in the bottle cap with the pointed tip of the scissors. Push the looped end of the string through the hole—from the inner surface of the cap out—until it's stopped by the second knot. Now, the loop sticking out of the cap will be what you use to hang the wind chime outdoors.

8. Thread the free end of the string through the bottle top. Then screw on the cap.

9. Tie the free end of the string hanging down through the middle of the bottle top around the remaining metal object. Adjust the length of the string so that when the center object moves, it strikes the objects in a ring around it. This will be the wind chime's ringer.

10. Hang the wind chime outdoors where it will catch a breeze.

BRAIN BOOSTER

There are two kinds of winds: local winds that affect only small areas and global winds that affect large areas. Both are caused by the sun's unequal heating of Earth's surface. Wherever the surface is warm, the air above it is heated and the air rises. As quickly as this air rises, cooler air rolls in to replace it. This moving air is wind. How strong the wind blows depends on how fast the heated air rises, letting cool air roll in. With the wind chime, you'll be able to hear whether the wind is just a gentle breeze or is strong and gusty.

BONUS PACK

On a day when the wind chimes tell you that the wind is strong, go for a walk. Watch for the wind at work, sculpting the world. Wind removes loose sand and dirt. Wind also moves sand and snow, piling it up into dunes and drifts.

Paint with a Pendulum ③

Investigate how a **pendulum**, a suspended weight, swings; then use one to make art. Before you start, take a look at a pendulum in action. Tie a string to a paper clip and tape a coin to the paper clip. Then hold the string in one hand, pull the weight back with the other hand, and let the weight go. That's a swinging pendulum.

FUEL UP

2 paper cups
hole punch
scissors
masking tape
sturdy string
red-colored sand (color it by mixing red food coloring into white sand)
blue-colored sand (color it by mixing blue food coloring into white sand)
standard-sized rubber band
tape
white glue
6 heavy books
white construction paper
newspapers
table

BLAST OFF!

1. Just below each cup's rim, use the hole punch to make 2 holes on opposite sides of the cup.

2. Use the scissors points to poke a small hole in the center bottom of each cup. Cover this with a piece of tape.

3. Cut a 6-inch (15-cm) piece of string for each cup. Tie one string through the holes in the top of each cup to make a handle.

4. Cut a 24-inch (60-cm) piece of string for each cup. Tie one string to the center of each cup's handle.

5. Fill one cup half full of red sand. Fill the other half full of blue sand.

6. Set the cups side by side and thread the free ends of each string through the rubber band. When you lift the cups by the strings, the rubber band now forms a ring around the two strings.

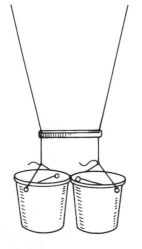

7. Tape the string for one cup to a tabletop (be sure you have an adult's permission to do this) or a chair seat. Position the cup so that it's hanging about 4 to 6 inches (10 to 15 cm) above the floor. If necessary, use a longer piece of string to make the pendulum longer.

8. Hang the second cup beside the first and at the same height. Be sure the strings are far enough apart so that the rubber band ring is stretched tight, rather than hanging loose. You may need a partner's help to do this.

9. Cover the floor under the cups with newspaper.

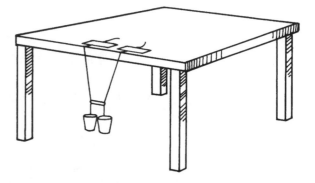

10. Place the paper on the newspaper directly under the cups and spread a thin layer of glue over the paper.

11. Have a partner help you quickly pull the tape off both cups.

12. Pull the red cup back just as far as the edge of the paper and let go. That will start this pendulum swinging.

13. Watch what happens. The sand raining down on the paper will stick, leaving a permanent record of the pendulum's swinging pattern.

14. About the time that the red cup stops swinging, the blue cup will start. Let the cups swing until both of them stop.

Brain Booster

A pendulum swings back and forth in an arc, but with each swing cycle, a little energy is conducted away through whatever the weight is attached to. Because a little energy is lost, the pendulum slows a little, so that each arc is a little shorter than the one before. For this art activity, you connected a pair of pendulums with a rubber band. The one that was swinging passed a little of the energy it lost to the other pendulum. Eventually, the pendulum losing energy lost so much that it almost stopped. Meanwhile, the other pendulum built up enough energy to start swinging. In turn, this second pendulum passed back some energy with each swing cycle. So the two pendulums traded off swinging until there wasn't enough energy left to propel either of them.

Bonus Pack

Go on a pendulum hunt. You'll be surprised at all of the pendulums you'll find, including these: a dangling earring, a pull chain, a bell's ringer, and a light hanging from a ceiling.

Make a Butterfly Bottle ③

Create a wind-powered work of art.

Fuel Up

clean, empty half-gallon (2-l) plastic bottle

colored markers

knife (for adult use only)

broom with wooden handle (or use a wooden dowel about 1 yard [0.9 m] long that will slide through the bottle's mouth)

hammer and nail (for adult use only)

Blast Off!

1. Remove the label from the bottle. Wash off any sticky residue and let the bottle dry.

2. Have a partner hold the bottle upside down. Use a black marker to draw a butterfly on the middle of the bottle. Make its body as thick as your thumb and the wings like flattened hearts on either side of the body.

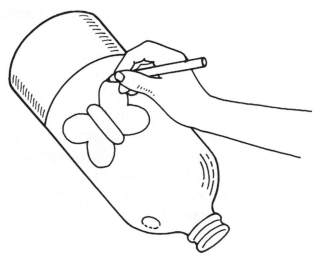

3. Have an adult use the knife to cut along the outer edge of each wing.

4. Fold each wing up until it is at a 90-degree angle to the butterfly's body. Then use the markers to color both sides of each wing. Color the butterfly's body black.

5. Repeat, making enough butterflies to circle the bottle.

6. Slide the broom handle into the bottle until it touches the bottom.

7. Have an adult tap the nail through the bottom of the bottle into the end of the broom handle. Be sure that the bottle can still turn freely.

8. Outdoors, hold the broom handle so that the wind catches the wings on the bottle.

Brain Booster

Sailboats were the earliest use of wind power. Then, as early as 200 B.C., farmers in China used sail-powered windmills to pump water. Later, farmers also used windmills to turn stones and grind grain. The first record of a windmill goes back to ancient Persia. It showed vertical sails that made the windmill go around the way the butterfly bottle spun. Later, the sails were attached to a disk that spun like a pinwheel in the wind. Until steam power and, later, the invention of electricity, wind energy was the best power source available. Today, windmills are at work again. This time, they are harnessing the wind's energy to generate electricity.

Bonus Pack

Brainstorm other shapes to catch the wind and make a bottle spin. Work with an adult to make other bottles, such as a bird bottle and a flower bottle.

That's Amazing!

Some windmills today are huge. Those at the Big Spring Wind Power Project in Big Spring, Texas, are 370 feet (112 m) tall and have rotors (the spinning blades) more than 216 feet (65 m) in diameter.

For More Science Art Fun

A Book of Artrageous Projects by Klutz Press (Palo Alto, Calif.: Klutz, Inc., 2000). Painting, making stained glass, embossing copper, and more—this book will inspire masterpieces. Ages 9–12.

Cooking Art: Easy Edible Art for Young Children by MaryAnn F. Kohn, Jean Potter, and Ronni Roseman-Hall (Beltsville, Md.: Gryphon House, 1997). Recipes even toddlers can help prepare, including many that require no baking. Ages 3–8.

Global Art: Activities, Projects and Inventions from around the World by MaryAnn F. Kohl and Jean Potter (Bellingham, Wash.: Bright Ring Publishing, 1998). Interesting, creative activities linked to cultures and countries. Ages 7–10.

Mudworks: Creative Clay, Dough, and Modeling Experiences by MaryAnn F. Kohl (Bellingham, Wash.: Bright Ring Publishing, 1992). There are 100 recipes designed for adults and children to enjoy together. Ages 4–8.

Nature's Art Box: From T-Shirts to Twig Baskets, 65 Cool Projects for Crafty Kids to Make with Natural Materials You Can Find Anywhere by Laura C. Martin (North Adams, Mass.: Storey Books, 2003). Illustrated, crafty activities that put nature to work, plus historical and cultural information. Ages 9–12.

Plants and Art Activities (Arty Facts) by Rosie McCormick (New York: Crabtree Publishing, 2002). Naturally, these activities get young artists involved with plants and the environment. Ages 7–10.

Science Arts: Discovering Science through Art Experiences by MaryAnn F. Kohl and Jean Potter (Bellingham, Wash.: Bright Ring Publishing, 1993). Ages 4–8. This book is packed with art experiments for adults to share with young children.

PART VII

Science Contests

Who can grow the tallest bean plants in just a week? What's the fastest way to melt ice? What kind of tool can you make that will let you hear whispers long distance? Who will design the fastest champion paper glider? These activities, and many more, will get family teams revved up and cheering each other on to victory. For even more fun, invite other families to compete against the home team.

CHAPTER 19

Biology Contests

Grow the Tallest Beans in a Week ❸

Discover what is needed for seeds to sprout, while you attempt to set the record for the tallest sprouts grown in just one week. Let every family member grow his or her own beans. Start by reading the What Plants Need to Grow box on page 244.

FUEL UP

Each contestant will need the following materials:

5 bean seeds (Use dried soup bean seeds; be sure every contestant has the same kinds of seeds and ones from the same bag.)

paper cup

water

pencil

potting soil (enough to fill the cup nearly full)

ruler

BLAST OFF!

1. Put the seeds in the paper cup and pour on enough water to cover. Let this sit overnight.

2. Dump out the water and use the pencil to punch three drainage holes in the bottom of the cup.

3. Fill the cup nearly full of potting soil.

> ## What Plants Need to Grow
>
> Seeds contain stored food that fuels a young plant's initial growth. Once that food supply is used up, the plant must begin producing its own food in its green leaves. Plants need water, soil, and sunlight to grow. Without sunlight, the young plants grow long and thin, using up their stored energy to generate stem growth. This response is a natural reaction that's designed to increase the sprout's chances of reaching sunlight.

4. Before planting the soaked seeds, each contestant should consider what seeds need to sprout and grow. Then contestants should think about what might be done to get the seeds to either sprout faster or grow taller faster once they sprout.

5. Contestants may use items that they find around the house to help them make their plants sprout and grow faster. First, contestants must share their ideas with an adult to be sure that what they want to do is safe to try.

6. Each contestant will plant just 3 of the 5 seeds, making sure that none are broken or missing their seed coats. The contestants should all plant their seeds on the same day.

7. At the end of 7 days after planting, each contestant will measure the height of the tallest plant in his or her pot.

8. The winner is the contestant with the tallest young plant.

9. Discuss what probably helped the young plant to grow so tall and whether this method will help the young plant keep on growing. Consider whether the method that started the plant growing might not be the best way to grow the plant to maturity.

BRAIN BOOSTER

At this initial growth stage, sprouting the seeds in a dark closet will make the plants grow taller faster. Adding fertilizer won't help plants grow faster because it won't help the seeds sprout, and once they have sprouted, the plants won't use the fertilizer until the stored food that was inside the seeds has been used up. Sprouts grown in the dark will win the tallest bean award but will die quickly unless they are placed in sunlight as soon as possible.

BONUS PACK

Put the bean plants in a warm, bright spot but not in full sun. Continue to water and watch the plants grow, blossom, and then produce one or more beans.

Grab It!

Experiment to see who has the fastest **reaction time**, the time it takes for the brain to analyze signals from the eyes and trigger a response.

FUEL UP

    partner
    ruler

BLAST OFF!

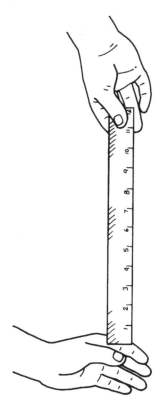

1. The partner should stand and hold the ruler vertically, with his or her fingers at the end with the highest number.

2. The player whose reaction time is being tested will stand beside the ruler with his or her hand around—but not touching—the end of the ruler with the lowest number. The player's thumb should be on the scale side of the ruler.

3. The partner will release the ruler within about 5 seconds, without signaling the player.

4. The player must grab the dropping ruler as quickly as possible. The player's reaction time is recorded in inches or centimeters— the point on the ruler that his or her thumb was closest to when the ruler was caught.

5. Play should rotate among all contestants. Each player should have three tries. The winner is the person with the fastest reaction time.

BRAIN BOOSTER

A player's reaction time may be speeded up by anticipation, the knowledge of what is about to happen, so that the person may begin the reaction process slightly before the partner actually releases the ruler. For the player to grab the ruler, the player's eyes must first see the falling ruler and send messages to the brain. Then the brain has to analyze this information and send a signal to the muscles of the arm and the hand, instructing them to move. To prevent anticipation from falsely affecting the reaction time, the partner should vary the release time. Then any player who grabs the ruler before it's released doesn't score during that round.

Bonus Pack

Divide players into teams, with girls and women versus boys and men or the youngest family members against the oldest. See which team has the fastest reaction time.

Take the Fewest Putts ③

Build a golf course and develop eye-hand coordination, while you play a game of miniature golf.

Fuel Up

    4 paper or Styrofoam cups
    egg cartons
    cereal boxes
    books
    toilet paper or paper towel tubes
    other optional items, such as boxes, stuffed toys, building blocks, pots, and pans
    permanent marker
    4 sheets notebook paper
    1 broom
    Ping-Pong balls (one per contestant)

Blast Off!

Get ready for the contest:

1. Build four holes to play. Get creative and brainstorm how each hole should be played. A cup laid on its side is the "hole" that the ball needs to reach. Each hole should include at least one obstacle to go around or two to go between. Holes may also include tunnels to roll through and ramps to go over. (Use egg cartons, cereal boxes, books, paper tubes, boxes, stuffed toys, building blocks, and pots and pans

to create obstacles and tunnels.) If the course is being created indoors, be sure that an adult agrees to the building plan.

2. Number the sheets of paper 1 through 4. Place one at the tee-off site for each hole.

3. Using the broom handle as the golf club and the Ping-Pong ball as the golf ball, test each hole during construction to be sure that it's possible to get the ball into the cup.

4. Number the balls so that each contestant has his or her own ball.

Compete:

1. The goal is to take as few strokes (swings at the ball) as possible to put the ball into the cup. Each contestant starts each hole at the tee-off site and travels toward the hole.

2. Each contestant scores one point for each stroke taken per hole.

3. Before swinging the club, each contestant should think about where the ball needs to go to get closer to the cup. Then the player should use the club to roll the ball closer and finally into the cup.

4. Contestants take turns hitting their balls toward the hole.

5. The winner is the contestant with the lowest score.

6. Discuss which playing strategies could be used to help players take the fewest number of strokes.

Brain Booster

Winning depends on eye-hand coordination and figuring out the most direct path to the hole. Eye-hand coordination is using what the eyes see to guide how the hands move to accomplish a task. This is a natural ability, but practice helps a person get better at specific tasks.

Bonus Pack

Create a hole that includes getting a ball past a swinging pendulum (a weight suspended from a string).

Build a Super Snooper ③

Divide the family into teams. Then tackle the challenge of building a tool to help a listener hear whispers across the longest possible distance.

FUEL UP

Each team will need the following materials:
    2 paper cups
    scissors
    6 feet (1.8 m) string
    funnel
    3 sheets paper
    masking tape

BLAST OFF!

1. Give the teams 5 minutes to brainstorm how to best use the materials to build a Super Snooper, a tool to amplify sound traveling through the air.

2. Give teams 10 minutes to construct their Super Snoopers.

3. Have each team choose one listener and blindfold that contestant. Give the listener the Super Snooper.

4. Have an adult stand at least 10 feet (3 m) away from the listener and make the following sounds at whisper level:
   ● Snap fingers.
   ● Whistle softly.
   ● Say "cat."
   ● Clap hands softly.
   ● Say "dog."

5. The listener should call out what sound he or she hears, and a score-keeper should record one point for each correct response.

6. If you'd like to do a second listening round, have each team select a second listener. This time, have the adult make five different animal sounds. The listener must correctly identify
   ● A cow—Mooo, Mooo
   ● A chicken—Cluck, Cluck
   ● A sheep—Baaa, Baaa

- A dog—Woof, Woof
- A pig—Oink, Oink

7. The winning team is the one with the highest score.

8. Allow time for each team to share how its Super Snooper was designed to help the listener hear sounds.

Brain Booster

Any method of collecting sound waves and funneling them into the ear will help. Sound happens when something vibrates, which starts the particles in the matter moving. The vibration creates a wave, similar to the waves on a body of water, that moves through the matter. The denser the matter is, the faster sound travels through it, so sound travels through water faster than through air and through a solid, like wood, faster than through water. Of course, sound isn't heard until sensors inside the human ear detect the sound waves and send messages to the brain; then the brain analyzes the messages.

Bonus Pack

Challenge teams to modify their Super Snoopers in any way, using materials found around the house. The challenge this time is to listen to the test sounds through a wall.

That's Amazing

Even a planet blowing up wouldn't produce any sound in space. There aren't enough gas molecules to create sound waves.

No More Duds ③

Divide the family into teams to tackle the challenge of popping corn with the fewest duds or unpopped kernels. Check out the Why Popcorn Pops box on page 250.

Fuel Up

hot air popper

Each team will need the following materials:

1 cup popcorn kernels—the popcorn for every team must come from the same source. If more than one bag is needed, mix bags together before distributing each team's cup of corn.

large mixing bowl

Why Popcorn Pops

A popcorn kernel is a seed that, if planted, is likely to sprout and grow into a new plant. Like any seed, the kernel contains stored starch, the food that would give the new plant energy to start growing. This stored starch is what becomes the popped corn. The stored starch also contains a little water. When this moisture reaches the boiling point for water (212°F/100°C), it turns into steam. Steam is a gas, and that means its molecules are farther apart than those in a liquid, so the steam takes up more space—enough to exert pressure and break open the tough seed coat. This break happens with such explosive force that the starch is blown up to as much as 40 times its original size. Even though the seed coat is tough, like any seed it has a tiny hole to let moisture enter at the time of sprouting. This opening also lets moisture escape. If a popcorn kernel gets too dry, it won't pop. Unpopped kernels are nicknamed duds.

BLAST OFF!

1. Give each team 5 minutes to figure out how it will make sure it has the fewest possible duds. Teams are also allowed the opportunity to use any other materials they can scavenge from around the house.

2. Give each team its materials and allow up to 1 hour's preparation time.

3. Hold the pop-off. Let each team pop its kernels, dividing them up into as many as four batches.

4. The winning team is the one with the fewest duds. Discuss why the winner probably won. Discuss what else might have been done to reduce the number of duds.

BRAIN BOOSTER

Any method that gets the kernels to absorb more moisture will help to reduce duds.

BONUS PACK

Let each team turn its test corn into a tasty treat by following one of these recipes.

Nutty Corn: In a saucepan, melt ¼ cup of creamy peanut butter and ¼ cup of margarine. Drizzle the peanut butter over the popped corn and toss in ½ cup of raisins.

Spicy Poppers: Sprinkle on 3 table-spoons of a powdered taco seasoning mix.

Sweet and Nice: Mix 1 teaspoon of ground cinnamon into ¼ cup of powdered sugar. Toss with popped corn.

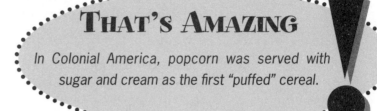

THAT'S AMAZING

In Colonial America, popcorn was served with sugar and cream as the first "puffed" cereal.

Grow Mold ASAP ②

Investigate what conditions encourage mold growth, while you compete to be the first person to grow mold. (Do not try this activity if anyone in the family is allergic to mold.) Read the What Is a Mold? box on this page before beginning.

FUEL UP

Each contestant will need:
    hammer and nail (for adult use only)
    clean, quart-sized (liter-sized) plastic container with large mouth and screw-on lid
    slices zucchini, cucumber, or cheese, and ½ slice bread
    water

BLAST OFF!

1. Have an adult use the hammer and nail to make about a half dozen holes in the container's lid.

2. Turn the container on its side.

3. Remove the lid and place the food items inside, so that they don't overlap.

4. Sprinkle water onto the food inside the jar.

5. Screw on the lid.

6. Brainstorm what could be done to speed up mold growth. Check with an adult to be sure what you want to try is safe to do and try it.

What Is a Mold?

Mold is a kind of living thing called a fungus. Unlike green plants that develop from seeds, molds and other kinds of fungus grow from tiny spores. These are so small, they blow in the wind, along with dust, and can get into almost any area that isn't well sealed. Like green plants, the molds need to be warm and wet to grow. But unlike green plants, molds don't make their own food. To grow, the mold feeds on bread, cheese, and other foods.

7. Watch for signs of furry mold growing on the food. The mold may be green, pink, yellow, or another color.

8. The winner is the first contestant to have mold growing on the food.

9. Discuss how the method that was used probably sped up mold growth. Consider what else could be tried to make mold grow even faster.

Brain Booster

Any conditions that allow the food to stay moist and warm will encourage mold growth.

Bonus Pack

Now hold this contest in reverse. Challenge all contestants to keep mold from growing for as long as possible. This will require creating conditions that don't favor mold growth, so the food will need to be kept cold, dry, and not exposed to air.

That's Amazing

One kind of fungus is a life-saver—penicillin. Alexander Fleming discovered that this fungus destroyed disease-causing bacteria. Penicillin was first used successfully to treat human patients in 1940. Penicillin proved so effective, it was called the "Miracle Drug."

Chemistry Contests

Keep Shiny Pennies from Turning Dark ③

First, follow the directions to make dark-colored pennies coppery bright. Also see the project "Make Dark Pennies Gleam" (see page 105). Then work as a family team to figure out how to make the pennies stay coppery. Start by reading the Why Pennies Lose Their Shine box on this page.

FUEL UP

5 dark-colored pennies (or any copper coins)
plate (or sturdy paper plate)
1 tablespoon salt
2 tablespoons vinegar
kitchen sink
paper towel

BLAST OFF!

1. Start by making the dark-colored pennies turn coppery bright. Place the pennies on the plate. Sprinkle salt over them. Pour on the vinegar. If any part of the pennies is still dark, repeat this process. Rinse the pennies in tap water at the kitchen sink and pat them dry with the paper towel.

Why Pennies Lose Their Shine

Pennies are made of copper. When copper comes in contact with the air, it changes to copper oxide, which appears dark in color. Rust forms on iron and steel in a similar way. Oxygen in the air reacts with the surface to create iron oxide, which appears as a reddish (rusty) color.

2. Brainstorm what could be done to stop the pennies from turning dark again.

3. Choose one idea to test. Check with an adult to be sure this idea is safe to try.

4. Have each team test its idea. Check for dark spots after 24 hours and again after 48 hours.

5. The winner is the team whose pennies have no dark spots. Or the winner is the team whose pennies have the largest area that's still coppery bright.

6. Have the winning team explain what it did. Discuss other methods that might work. Test any ideas that an adult agrees are safe to try.

Brain Booster

Salt contains chloride atoms. When these chloride atoms are present in a weak acid solution, such as vinegar, they cause the copper compounds on the pennies to dissolve easily. As these compounds move into the vinegar solution, a fresh, shiny layer of copper becomes visible. Any method that keeps the surface of the pennies from coming in contact with the air will keep them from turning dark again. One way would be to coat the pennies with petroleum jelly. Another would be to paint them with clear fingernail polish.

Bonus Pack

Divide the family into teams to tackle this challenge: keep steel wool from rusting.

Keep the Reaction Going ②

Discover how an acid and a base interact, while you meet this challenge. Before you start, read the information in the Acids and Bases box on page 255.

Fuel Up

Each team will need the following materials:
  clear plastic cup
  water

teaspoon
measuring spoons
baking soda
vinegar
clock with a second hand

BLAST OFF!

1. Divide into teams.

2. Watch the basic reaction before brainstorming.

3. Basic Reaction: Fill a cup two-thirds full of water and stir in 1 tablespoon of baking soda. Add 3 tablespoons of vinegar. The interaction of the baking soda and the vinegar causes a bubbling reaction. Record for how many seconds bubbles are produced.

4. The goal is to make the reaction continue longer *without* adding any more baking soda or vinegar. Other household items and chemicals may be added. Have the family teams brainstorm what could be done and choose one idea to try. Check with an adult to be sure the team's idea is safe to try.

5. Compete. Time how long bubbles are produced.

6. The winning team is the one that makes the reaction produce bubbles for the longest time.

7. Discuss any strategy that might be used to keep the reaction happening even longer. Check with an adult and, if this is safe to do, try it.

Acids and Bases

There are two important groups of matter called acids and bases. Because of their chemical structure, acids and bases have very different properties. Bases, by their nature, tend to make good cleaning agents. They are most often found in soaps and detergents. Baking soda is one of the few bases that's used to produce foods. Acids are naturally found in some foods, such as fruits, vinegar, and milk. These acids give the food their distinct, slightly bitter, taste. When an acid and a base come into contact with each other, these two kinds of matter interact. A chemical change occurs, and in the process, carbon dioxide gas is released. If the reaction is happening in a liquid, such as water, the escaping gas appears as bubbles.

Brain Booster

Adding another base or an acid will keep the reaction going. Common bases that are found around the house include ammonia, borax, milk of magnesia, detergents, and powdered soaps. Numerous foods contain acids, including fruit juices, tea, and milk. Baking powder, which contains both baking soda and a dry, powdered acid called cream of tartar, would renew the reaction by supplying both the base and the acid.

Bonus Pack

Use the baking soda and vinegar reaction to make Honeycomb Candy. You'll need: ½ pound (226 g) of granulated sugar, 2 tablespoons of clear vinegar, 2 tablespoons of honey, ¼ pint (118 ml) of water, and ¼ teaspoon of baking soda. Grease four cups of a muffin pan. Put the sugar, vinegar, honey, and water into a saucepan. Have an adult bring this mixture to a boil while stirring with a wooden spoon. Boil and stir for 3 minutes. Remove from the heat and immediately add the baking soda. Stir until the mixture looks creamy. Divide the mixture between the four cups. Let it sit until hard. Then pop the Honeycomb Candy out of the muffin tin, break into pieces, and enjoy.

Hot Stuff ③

Make one kind of matter, ice, change to a liquid—water—as quickly as possible.

Fuel Up

  timer or clock with a second hand
  sieve
  measuring cup

Each team will need a set of these materials:

  6 ice cubes in a self-sealing plastic bag (Be sure the teams have ice cubes made from exactly the same amount of water.)
  3 sheets newspaper
  4 paper towels
  oven mitts
  rock

Blast Off!

1. Divide the family into teams.

2. Explain that heat energy makes ice melt or change from its solid form into liquid water.

3. Give the teams 3 minutes to brainstorm a list of possible ways to speed up how fast ice cubes melt and choose one to try.

   Note: Teams must leave the ice in its bag and are limited to using the materials provided.

4. Next, give each team its materials and allow the team 2 minutes to make the ice cubes melt as much as possible.

5. To determine the amount melted, each team will pour the water in its bag through the sieve into the measuring cup.

6. The winner is the team that melted all of its ice cubes first or the team that produced the most water within the time limit.

Brain Booster

Breaking up the ice cubes into smaller pieces will speed up how quickly they melt because it will increase the amount of surface area that's exposed to heat. Heat causes the water to change from its solid state to its liquid state. This happens because heat energy makes the water molecules speed up. Friction, or rubbing, is one source of heat energy. So is light energy. Another source is the human body because it uses food energy to generate heat energy. The smaller the bits of matter, the faster the heat energy is able to speed up all of the molecules and change the solid ice to liquid water.

Bonus Pack

Melt ice to make a tasty treat—sherbet. For a family-sized batch, combine one 11-ounce (311-g) can of mandarin oranges; one 6-ounce (170-g) can of frozen orange juice concentrate, partially thawed; one 14-ounce (396-g) can of sweetened condensed milk; and a half-gallon (2-l) bottle of orange soft drink. Put the ingredients into an electric or hand-crank ice cream–making machine. Follow the machine's directions to surround the center cylinder with layers of crushed ice and rock salt. Once the mixture is frozen, enjoy.

Note: If an ice cream maker is not available, pour ½ cup of the liquid into separate self-sealing plastic sandwich bags. Then place these inside a large self-sealing bag and pack layers of crushed ice and rock salt around the small bags. The big bag will need to be shaken until the mixture becomes thickened—about 15 minutes.

Chill Out! ③

This time, discover how insulation can help to block heat and keep ice from melting. The team that can hang on to its ice for the longest time wins.

Fuel Up

    timer or clock with second hand
    sieve
    measuring cup
Each team will need a set of these materials:
    6 ice cubes
    large self-sealing plastic bag
    3 sheets newspaper
    aluminum foil
    wool sock or mitten
    bag full of dirt

Blast Off!

1. Divide the family into teams. Explain that an **insulator** is anything that will block the transfer of energy. Brainstorm together all the possible ways to use the available materials to keep heat energy from reaching the ice cubes.

2. Give the teams 3 minutes to brainstorm possible ways to slow down how fast ice cubes melt and choose one to try. Teams must leave the ice in its bag and are limited to using the materials provided.

3. Have all the teams set up their materials to insulate their ice cubes.

4. Wait 15 minutes before checking how much the ice cubes have melted. To make this a bigger challenge, require the teams to keep the ice from melting for up to an hour.

5. To determine the amount melted, each team will pour the water in the team's bag through the sieve into the measuring cup.

6. The winner is the team that produces the least amount of water.

Brain Booster

Any method that blocks heat from reaching the ice will slow melting. Some materials let heat energy pass through more readily than others do. Layering materials can also make them better insulators because air is trapped in-between. Air is a good insulator because air particles are far apart, so less heat is transferred through air than through a solid, such as a metal. One method of insulating the ice would be to put the small bag inside the big one, blow into the bag to fill it with air, and seal it. Wrapping wool and/or layers of paper around the small bag would add to its insulating effect.

Bonus Pack

Find out why walruses, seals, and whales that live in the cold Arctic Ocean have a thick layer of blubber or fat. Fill a large self-sealing plastic bag half full of lard or margarine. Have a team member put his or her hand into another clean plastic bag. Next, have that person push his or her bagged hand into the bag of lard or margarine. Then have that person put the hand surrounded by the bag of lard or margarine into a sink full of ice water. At the same time have the person put his or her bare hand into the ice water. Ask the test person to describe how much colder the bare hand feels—a little, some, or a lot colder. It will feel a lot colder. Fat, as well as lard or margarine, is a good insulator.

CHAPTER 21

Physics Contests

Make a Sheet of Paper Stronger ③

Investigate how to make a sheet of notebook paper support as many pennies as possible. In the process, discover that some shapes are stronger than others.

FUEL UP

Each team will need the following materials:

enough books to make 2 supporting towers at least 5 inches (12.5 cm) high (or you can substitute cereal boxes)

1 sheet notebook paper

30 pennies (or substitute other coins that are all identical)

*tape (this item is used in the Brain Booster section)

*scissors (this item is used in the Brain Booster section)

BLAST OFF!

1. Divide the family into teams.

2. Have each team build two supporting towers at least 5 inches (12.5 cm) high and about 5 inches (12.5 cm) apart.

3. Have each team place the sheet of notebook paper as a bridge spanning the two towers.

4. Then have each team place coins on the center of the paper bridge until it collapses.

5. Allow each team 5 minutes to brainstorm ways, using the available materials, to change the notebook paper bridge to make it strong enough to support more pennies.

6. Give the teams 10 minutes to test their ideas prior to competing.

7. Have each team display its method for making the paper bridge stronger. Have the teams demonstrate how many pennies their bridges will hold before collapsing.

8. The winning team is the one whose paper bridge will support the greatest number of pennies.

9. Discuss what made the winning bridge strong.

Brain Booster

Any method that changes the shape of the paper to create triangles (accordion folding the paper), arches (rolling and taping the paper into a tube), or rectangles (folding and taping the paper into a box shape) will make it stronger. These shapes are used to build big structures like skyscrapers and bridges. They are also shapes that make it possible to have strength without a lot of weight. These shapes are best able to withstand the compression force of a weight.

Bonus Pack

Tackle this new challenge. Use a sheet of paper to carry water at least 6 feet (1.8 m). The winner is the team that finds a way to fold the paper to create a pocket that will hold water. One way is to fold the paper in half diagonally. Then fold the right-hand and left-hand corners to the middle and fold the upper points down. Carefully open the middle of the folded paper to create a cup and pour in the water.

Build a Champion Paper Glider ③

Divide the family into teams. Start by building identical gliders to fly. Then get creative and modify the gliders to stay airborne for the longest possible time. First, check out the How a Glider Works box on page 262.

How a Glider Works

The paper glider, like any glider, is propelled by *thrust*—the forward movement given at launch time. If the shape causes the air to move faster over the top of the wing, the glider also has a certain amount of lift. That's because the faster-moving air on top of the wing has less push than the slower-moving air below does. *Drag*, the resistance of moving through the air, slows the glider down. Gravity pulls on everything, but because the glider is light, it drops slowly. Thrust, lift, drag, and gravity are at work when a glider flies. Thrust and lift get the glider airborne. Eventually, drag will slow the glider to the point that gravity takes over. Then the glider drops to the ground and the flight is over.

Fuel Up

clock with a second hand
Each contestant or team will need the following materials:
sheet of plain white typing paper
standard-sized steel paper clip

Blast Off!

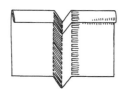

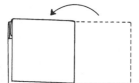

1. Build the basic glider by following these steps:

   ● Fold one long edge of the paper over about ½ inch (1.25 cm) and crease.

   ● Repeat this fold three more times.

   ● Bring the two short ends of the paper together to fold in half. Crease.

   ● To form one wing, fold back about 1 inch (2.5 cm) from the center fold and crease.

   ● Flip the glider over and form the other wing the same way.

   ● Hold the glider with the folded edge down. Slip the paper clip over the folded edge to hold the two sides together.

   ● Fold up about ½ inch (1.25 cm) at either wing edge.

2. Test the basic glider with an overhand throw. Time how many seconds it stays airborne. Test it at least three times.

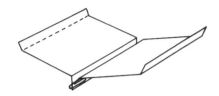

3. Brainstorm ways to modify the glider to make it stay airborne longer. Anything can be used, except a motor.

4. Check your modification plans with an adult to be sure they are safe to test.

5. Make modifications to the glider.

6. Hold a family glider challenge. Have each team fly its glider three times and add together the seconds it stays airborne each time.

7. The champion is the team whose glider has the longest total time in the air.

8. Discuss other modifications that might make the gliders stay airborne even longer.

Brain Booster

Anything that decreases the glider's drag or resistance as it pushes through the air will let it stay airborne longer.

Bonus Pack

Test other modifications to build a glider that can stay airborne even longer than the current champ. Hold a rematch.

Make a Water-Producing Box ②

This challenge will really take some brainpower. The goal is to use the materials provided to make a box that appears to yield twice as much water as is poured into it. Here's a clue—start by figuring out a way to store water in the box so that adding just a little more will trigger this reservoir to empty.

Fuel Up

measuring cup
Every team will need the following materials:
half-gallon (2-l) plastic bottle
scissors with a sharp point

cardboard box big enough to hide the bottle after its top is removed
ruler
permanent marking pen
2 feet (0.6 m) of ½-inch (1.25-cm) flexible plastic tubing (such as is used for aquarium pumps)
kitchen sink

Blast Off!

1. Divide the family into teams or compete against other family teams.

2. Brainstorm which strategy might work to meet the challenge.

3. Choose a strategy for building a Water-Producing Box. Check with an adult to be sure this strategy is safe to try.

4. Construct the Water-Producing Box to test it.

5. Start by pouring 1 cup of water into the Water-Producing Box. Measure how many cups of water pour out.

6. The winning team is the one whose box produces the most cups of water.

7. Have the winning team explain how its Water-Producing Box works. Discuss anything that could be done to make the box produce even more water once 1 cup is poured in.

Brain Booster

This challenge can be met by creating a reservoir full of water inside the box. Then the end of the tube inside the box is just above the water level, and the end outside the box is below the water level. Pouring a cup of water into the reservoir brings the water level up to the tube and that causes the reservoir to start draining. Since the reservoir holds more than a cup of water, the box appears to yield more than double what was poured in.

Bonus Pack

Make the box appear to change the water's color. For example, when clear water is poured in, red water flows out. This can be done by adding food coloring to the water in the box's reservoir.

Make the Longest Water Stream ③

The challenge this time is to make water spurt out the farthest from a hole in a leaky can. Feel the pressure? So will the water in this contest.

Fuel Up

scissors with sharp point
3 half-gallon (2-l) plastic bottles
sturdy tape
ruler
sink

Blast Off!

1. Tackle this as a family. The challenge is to make a hole in the bottle that will produce the longest spurt of water, without squeezing the bottle.

2. Brainstorm what might work to make water spurt out the farthest. Don't forget that water has weight. To prove it, lift a plastic bottle full of water and an empty bottle.

3. Choose three ideas to test. Be sure an adult agrees that these ideas will be safe to test.

4. Use the scissors to drill a hole in the bottle.

5. Cover the hole with tape while you fill the bottle in the sink.

6. Remove the tape and immediately have a team member use the ruler to measure how far the water spurts from the bottle.

7. The winning idea is the one that makes the water spurt the farthest.

8. Discuss what else might make the water spurt farther and test it.

Brain Booster

Putting a hole as near as possible to the bottom of the bottle will make the water spurt farthest. Because water has weight, the water pushing down makes the pressure greatest at the bottom of the water column.

BONUS PACK

Figure out a way to increase the water pressure inside the bottle to make the water spurt out even farther. One idea that would work is to squeeze the bottle.

Make the Longest Circuit ③

Investigate what kinds of materials are good conductors of electricity, while you build the longest possible circuit from recycled objects.

FUEL UP

measuring tape

scissors

Each team will need the following materials:

12-inch (30-cm) long by 2-inch (5-cm) wide strip of aluminum foil

table

transparent tape

D-cell battery

1.5-volt flashlight bulb

12 steel paper clips

5 copper pennies (or other copper coins)

BLAST OFF!

1. Place the foil on a table, dull side up. Stick strips of tape down the length of the foil. Cut out the strips.

2. Fold the foil strips in half lengthwise, with the taped side inside. Crease.

3. To test the basic circuit, sit the flat end of the D-cell battery on one end of a strip of foil. Wrap the free end of the foil strip around the light bulb's base. Touch the tip of the bulb to the knob end of the D-cell. This should light up. If it doesn't, try a different battery or bulb.

4. To launch the challenge, have an adult snip each team's foil into two short pieces. The challenge is to make the longest circuit possible, using only the paper clips, the pennies, and anything the team members have on them to connect the two pieces of foil.

5. Allow the teams 5 to 10 minutes to tackle this challenge. Contestants will need to test items to see what conducts electricity to light the bulb.

6. Use the measuring tape to decide the winning team.

Brain Booster

Any good conductor or material that lets an electric current flow through easily can be added to the circuit. How long a team can make its circuit depends on the team's creativity and objects that are available. Most metals, such as steel, copper, gold, aluminum, and silver, are good conductors. These are used for coins, the frames for glasses, jewelry, dental appliances, and lots more. Graphite—what is commonly called pencil lead—is also a good conductor of electricity.

Bonus Pack

Have the family members try to make the longest circuit possible out of all of the pennies they can collect around the house. Then see who has the most cents.

Make Bubbles Last Longest ③

Explore what affects evaporation, the process of a liquid changing into a gas, and tackle the challenge of keeping soap bubbles from popping.

Fuel Up

Every team will need the following materials:

   1 straw
   1 cup Super Bubble Brew (see the recipe in the box on page 268)
   1 disposable aluminum pie pan

Blast Off!

1. Divide the family into teams.

2. Have the teams blow bubbles by inserting straws into the bubble solution (in the pie pan) and blowing gently. Each team should watch its bubbles until they pop and watch what happens to the soap film.

The teams should see colors in the soap film appear to flow down. This shows that the solution is losing water through evaporation, or the liquid is changing into a gas and is moving into the air.

3. Have the teams list everything that could make the water evaporate from the bubble solution. Then have them brainstorm ways to keep the water from evaporating.

4. The teams will need to scavenge any materials they think they could use to slow their bubbles from evaporating.

5. Give each team three tries to test its bubble-saving strategy. Then have each team compute the average time its bubbles lasted. (To compute the average: add together the results for each test, then divide by the total number of tests.)

6. The winning team is the one whose bubbles lasted the longest before popping.

BRAIN BOOSTER

Anything that decreases airflow around the bubble will slow the evaporation rate. One possibility is shielding the bubble with a paper wall. A soap bubble is a film of soap solution filled with air. The soap solution is made up of water molecules sandwiched between layers of soap molecules. The soap dries fastest where the layer of soap is thinnest, or stretched the most. Then the water evaporates, and the remaining layer of soap is too thin to contain the air pressure inside, so the bubble pops.

BONUS PACK

Use the straw to see who can blow the biggest bubble. To measure a bubble, let it break against a sheet of paper and measure the distance across the wet spot that the bubble created. Or have the teams compete to see which one can blow the tallest tower of bubbles.

Super Bubble Brew

Mix together ⅓ cup of water, ⅓ cup of dish-washing liquid (Dawn or Joy work best), and 1 tablespoon of glycerin (available at most grocery stores or pharmacies). The glycerin helps to keep the bubble from drying out quickly, so that the bubble lasts longer. You can substitute corn syrup for glycerin, but glycerin works better.

Make a Sinker Float ③

Investigate **buoyancy**, the tendency of objects to float in a gas or a liquid, while you compete to make a ball of clay sink as little as possible.

FUEL UP

Each team will need the following materials:
  scissors
  half-gallon (2-l) plastic bottle
  water
  Ping-Pong-ball-sized lump of modeling clay
  toothpick (or substitute a pencil with a sharp point)
  ruler

BLAST OFF!

1. Divide the family into teams.

2. Have an adult from each team use scissors to cut the top off the team's plastic bottle and fill it two-thirds full of water. Next, have each team gently place its ball of clay in the water to see it sink.

3. The challenge for each team is to make the clay buoyant, meaning that it will sink as little as possible. Give the teams 2 minutes to brainstorm how to make this happen.

4. The teams should check the idea they want to test with an adult to be sure it's safe to try.

5. Give each team 10 minutes to collect any needed supplies and prepare to compete.

6. Have each team place its clay ball in its test bottle. When the water stops moving, have someone scratch a mark on the clay at the water line.

7. The winner is the team with the smallest amount of clay underwater.

8. Ask the winning team to explain the strategy it used to make its clay buoyant. Discuss what else might work even better. If it's safe to test, try it.

BRAIN BOOSTER

Two winning strategies will make the clay buoyant: (1) transforming the clay into a buoyant shape; (2) making the water denser. For example, the clay could be changed into a boat shape, or salt or sugar could be added to the water to make it denser. An object is buoyant when the force of the water pushing up is greater than the force of the object pushing down. Buoyancy happens because an object displaces, or pushes aside, enough water to support it. If you have ever seen the water level rise when you got into the bathtub, you have witnessed this displacement. One way to make an object more buoyant is to change its shape so that it displaces more water. Another way is to add "floaters" attached to the object. Because these also displace water, the floaters help to support the object. A denser liquid pushes up more, so that things are more buoyant in it. That's why things float more easily in saltwater than in freshwater, and they float best in really salty water like the Great Salt Lake in Utah.

Bonus Pack

Challenge the teams to make a boat that will support the most pennies (or marbles) without sinking.

For More Science Contests Fun

Planting the Seed: A Guide to Gardening by Suzanne Winckler (Minneapolis, Minn.: Lerner Publishing Group, 2002). Color photos and drawings bring to life information about plants and gardens. The emphasis is on organic gardening. Ages 8–14.

Roots, Shoots, Buckets & Boots: Gardening Together with Children by Sharon Lovejoy (New York: Workman Publishing Company, 1999). This book contains lots of gardening lore, ideas, and activities. Ages 7–10.

The Everything Kids' Science Experiments Book: Boil Ice, Float Water, Measure Gravity—Challenge the World around You! by Tom Mark Robinson (Carmel, Calif.: Adams Media Corporation, 2001). This book encourages inventive thinking and includes activities that can be done with household items. Ages 9–12.

The Mad Scientist Handbook: The Do-It-Yourself Guide to Making Your Own Rock Candy, Anti-Gravity Machine, Edible Glass, Rubber Eggs, Fake Blood, Green Slime, and Much Much More by Joey Green (New York: Perigee, 2000). A collection of creepy crafts and quirky experiments that are guaranteed to intrigue. Ages 8 and up.

You Gotta Try This! Absolutely Irresistible Science by Vicki Cobb (New York: HarperCollins, 1999). This book contains 50 fascinating experiments for curious kids. Ages 9–12.

Science Words

acid   A kind of chemical that reacts with a base. Some kinds of acids corrode or break down metals. Weak acids give certain foods, such as lemons, a sour taste.

air pressure   The downward force exerted by the weight of the overlying air.

bark   The outer protective covering on trees.

base   A kind of chemical that reacts with an acid. The traits of bases often make them good cleansers. One kind of base that's found in foods is baking soda.

buoyancy   The tendency of objects to float in a gas, like air, or a liquid, like water.

camouflage   Concealing something by disguising it to look like its surroundings.

capillary action   The movement of a liquid through a porous material, due to the liquid's attraction to the material and the attraction of the liquid's molecules to one another.

carbon dioxide   A gas in the air that is used by plants during photosynthesis or food production. Also, a waste gas given off by animals.

cell   The building block of all plants and animals.

center of gravity   The point around which a body's or an object's weight is evenly distributed in all directions.

centrifugal force   The action that moves molecules outward from a center point.

chemical change   Altering the molecular structure of one type of matter, making it into a different kind of matter.

chlorophyll   The green coloring matter produced in plants that helps them use the sun's energy to produce food.

classifying   Assigning objects, events, or living things to groups.

condensation   The process of a gas's molecules slowing down enough to become a liquid.

consumer   Any living thing that takes food energy from another living thing.

crystal   A solid that's made up of atoms in a set pattern.

density   The measurement of the mass of something, how much matter it contains, and how much space it takes up, compared to its volume (the three dimensional space it's in).

depth perception   The ability to see objects within a visual field, especially to see them in three dimensions.

diffusion   The process of something spreading out from where there is a lot of it to where there is very little.

dissolve   The process whereby something breaks up into smaller bits that are suspended in a liquid.

drag   The force of resistance caused by one thing moving against something else.

electrons   Charged particles that orbit the nucleus of an atom.

evaporate   The process of a liquid's molecules speeding up enough to become a gas.

food chain   Food energy produced by green plants being passed on from consumer to consumer.

friction   The resistance created by an object rubbing against something. It will cause an object to slow down and may cause it to stop.

gravity   The force of attraction between Earth or another body in the universe on an object on or near its surface.

habitat   The place in the world that supplies the amount of water, the kinds of food, and the shelter needed for the plants and the animals that live there.

insulator   Something that reduces or prevents the transmission of heat, electricity, or sound.

lift   The force that's great enough to overcome an object's weight and push it upward.

liquid   A kind of matter that has a definite weight but whose shape can change easily.

magnifier   Something that causes objects to appear larger than they actually are.

matter   Any substance or material.

melting point   The temperature at which a solid becomes a liquid.

molecules   The smallest bit of something that can exist and still have all of its characteristics.

momentum   The property of a moving object that keeps it in motion. How far and how fast an object moves is determined by the object's weight and speed.

orbit   The particular path one thing follows when going around something else, such as Earth going around the sun.

pendulum   A suspended weight.

persistence of vision   The process of vision in which the brain, while analyzing messages received from light-sensitive cells in the eye, retains an image for a split second.

photosynthesis   The process by which green plants produce food from carbon dioxide and water in the presence of light energy.

phototropism   The response of an organism to light, as when plants grow toward light.

physical change   Changes to the structure of something, such as to its size and shape, but not to its chemical makeup.

pigment   Coloring matter.

polymer   A naturally occurring or man-made material made up of large molecules that are chains of linked-together smaller molecules.

potential energy   Stored energy.

predator   A living thing that catches animals in order to eat them.

prey   Living things that are caught by predators.

producer   A living thing that makes food energy.

qualitative   Related to the special features that something has, such as its color or texture, which can be observed by using the senses of sight, touch, smell, taste, and hearing.

quantitative   Related to the specific measurement of something, such as its weight or length, which can be observed by using special instruments, such as a ruler, a balance scale, and a thermometer.

reaction time   The time between a stimulus and a response.

refraction   The bending of light waves that happens when they change speed, such as when they pass from air into water.

scavenger   A consumer that eats dead plants or animals.

solid   A kind of matter with a definite weight and shape. Its shape can't change easily.

static electricity   Electrons or charged bits that are collected in one place, rather than flowing from one place to another.

surface tension   Molecules at the surface of a liquid that cling together to create a sort of "film."

thrust   A force that pushes something or somebody.

trait   A characteristic or a feature that can be used to identify something or somebody.

trajectory   The path of a moving object. It's affected by the forces of thrust, friction, and gravity.

vibrations   Movements of molecules that follow the same path over and over.

water vapor   The gas state of water.

weathering   The breakdown of rocks due to the action of natural forces, such as wind and water.

wind   Moving air.

Index